Annual Indonesia Lecture Series

number 25

Horizons of home:
nation, gender and migrancy in island Southeast Asia

edited by

Penelope Graham

Monash Asia Institute

Clayton

Monash University Press

Monash University

Victoria 3800

Australia

www.monash.edu.au/mai

© Monash Asia Institute 2008

National Library of Australia cataloguing-in-publication entry:

Title: Horizons of home : nation, gender and migrancy in island
             Southeast Asia / edited by Penelope Graham.

ISBN: 1876924292

Series: Annual Indonesia lecture series ; no. 25.

Notes: Bibliography.

Subjects: Citizenship--Indonesia
             Citizenship--East Timor.
             Migration, Internal--Indonesia
             Migration, Internal--East Timor.

             Graham, Penelope.

             304.809598

Printed by Filmshot Graphics Pty Ltd, Ringwood, Victoria, Australia.

Contents

About the contributors

Penny Graham is Head of the Anthropology program, Monash University. She is also Director of the Centre of Southeast Asian Studies in the Monash Asia Institute and Executive Director of the Monash University Herb Feith Foundation. She has research interests in Indonesia and Malaysia, including labour migration and life narratives of social and cultural change.

Sara Graham is an honours graduate of the Anthropology program at Monash University, where she received a Monash Vice-Chancellor's award for her honours year and is a research associate with an interest in Timorese-Chinese in Melbourne. Sara and Penny are not related.

Graeme Hugo is University Professorial Research Fellow, Professor of the Department of Geographical and Environmental Studies and Director of the National Centre for Social Applications of Geographic Information Systems at the University of Adelaide.

Claire Kelly is an honours graduate of the Anthropology program at Monash University, where she is a research associate with interests in international migration, globalisation and feminist political theory. She also works with a non-government organisation concerned with trafficking in women to Australia for prostitution.

Janet Penny is a research associate with the Centre of Southeast Asian Studies, Monash Asia Institute, Monash University, with long-standing research interests in Indonesia and Indonesians in Australia.

Riwanto Tirtosudarmo is Director of the Centre for Social and Cultural Studies, Indonesian Institute of Sciences (PMB-LIPI), Jakarta, Indonesia, and is a visiting scholar with the Centre of Southeast Asian Studies, Monash University.

Catharina Purwani Williams is a visiting fellow at the School of Physical, Environmental and Mathematical Sciences, UNSW@ADFA, Australian Defence Force Academy, Canberra. She lectures in Geography on population, resources and development in Asia Pacific.

Phillip Winn is a lecturer with the School of Archaeology and Anthropology at the Australian National University in Canberra. He is currently involved in research concerning Muslim diversity in eastern Indonesia, in addition to interests in emerging political cultures, communal conflict and post-conflict situations.

Home and homeland: nation, gender and migrancy in island Southeast Asia

Penelope Graham

As familiar words in everyday language, the ideas of 'home' and 'homeland' hide their complexities well. In a series of articles published in the 1990s, Liisa Malkki notes how commonsense ideas relating people to place—roots, land, country, nations and national identity—focus our attention on 'what it means to be rooted in a place' (Malkki 1992:25–6). As taken-for-granted ways of thinking, she argues, these metaphors incline us to conceptualise identity in spatial terms, such that journalists, scholars and policy-makers alike tend to depict the natural human condition as being 'emplaced' rather than 'displaced'. If the concept of 'roots' links identity to territory, the same is true, she suggests, of the other major metaphor for community, 'blood' (Malkki 1992:27, n7). Whether the emphasis is on kinship or home (motherland, fatherland, homeland), all these metaphors similarly naturalise the links between people and place, she argues, as if 'each nation is a grand genealogical tree, rooted in the soil that nourishes it' (Malkki 1992:28). In her view, this tree motif evokes both temporal continuity and territorial rootedness.

Tree symbolism and botanical metaphors are not, of course, limited to the discourse of the nation. Tree images—root and branch—are relied on by the Yolngu people of northeastern Arnhem Land to serve as 'a symbol of the relations of one group to many others and of the distinct identity of the group' (Keen 1994:169). Botanical metaphors are also regularly invoked among Austronesian-speaking populations to represent relationships of similarity and difference. Indeed, James Fox (1997a:17) argues that tree imagery is 'near universal' for such purposes. As ethnographic accounts of tree symbolism indicate that trees represent images of continuity and reproduction, in contrast to images of change and destruction (Rival 1998), so trees may feature in metaphorical connections linking them to human bodies, generational continuity and clan territories (Bonnemère 1998). Tree symbolism thus lends itself to the symbolic representation of forms of human collectivity with temporal and spatial dimensions.

Besides ordinary language and nationalist discourses, Malkki analyses mid- to late 20th-century scholarly studies of nations, nationalism and refugees to reveal their tendency to privilege the territorialised aspect of human experience. Influenced by these ways of thinking, she suggests, we come to see nationalism, or as she terms it, 'the national order of things', as if it were 'the natural order of things' (Malkki 1995a:508). This includes a proclivity to view being 'uprooted' from a national community as 'automatically to lose one's identity, traditions and culture'. Such thinking, Malkki criticises as being imbued with a 'sedentarist analytical bias'. Her strategy for overcoming this bias is to stop treating 'displacement' and its flipside 'emplacement' as analytically distinct. These processes should in her view be seen as linked historical products, always unfinished. What is required is research that does not 'assume the purity or naturalness, wholeness or wholesomeness of origins, identities, communities, cultural traditions or nationalities' (Malkki 1995a:516).

Her own detailed and subtle ethnographic research on refugees in African contexts demonstrates the merits of this approach. In an important study that was published as genocide was unfolding in Rwanda, she explored how diverse experiences of exile generated quite distinct constructions of national identity and 'homeland' among two groups of Hutu refugees inhabiting quite different settings in Tanzania. These Hutu had fled massacres in Burundi in 1972. In Tanzania, some were settled in an isolated refugee camp, while others lived dispersed in the more fluid environment of a township. Her most striking research finding is that while the camp refugees developed a heightened sense of being a nation-in-waiting, intently focused on the moral trajectory of reclaiming their 'homeland', those refugees living in town tended to seek ways of assimilating and developing multiple situational identities, such that their 'homeland' Burundi was not a moral destination, but simply a place (Malkki 1992; 1995b).

When it comes to ordinary language encoding the link between identity and territory, Malkki's analysis is not without its critics. Sanjay Srivastava (2005:382, n8), for instance, suggests that 'at least for Indian society, there is a considerable body of long-standing, "ordinary", discourse about the complexities of belonging'. For the Indian case, Srivastava (2005:384) explores two parallel discourses of 'home' and belonging, to argue that the one which focuses on itinerancy has been marginalised in favour of the one 'which views Indian society as essentially "attached" to localities and has conflated mobility with highways and railways'. This latter discourse, which he suggests articulates a wider temporal sensibility, has naturalised 'the historical invention of "home" in the Indian context as a fixed idea' and entrenched this notion in the perspectives of modern social science, at the expense of the parallel discourse, which he argues is really 'about space, and about the linkage of spaces in social life'.

This idea of the linkage of spaces through 'wandering' as a trope in Indian society is reminiscent of the more formal ordering of places characteristic of eastern Indonesia. James Fox (1997b) has pointed out that, among Austronesian-speaking populations, recitation of 'topogeny' (the ordered succession of place names, often describing a journey through the landscape) is as common as 'genealogy' (the ordered succession of personal names) as a mnemonic device for tracing origins that establish social or ritual precedence among people or groups. He notes also that some Austronesian societies give preference to topogeny over genealogy, while others rely on both of these forms as ordering structures but use them in differing contexts.

As Liisa Malkki's work drew out the analytical consequences of a bias towards territorialising concepts of identity, so it lent weight to calls through the 1990s for anthropologists to pay greater attention to 'moving targets' (Breckenridge & Appadurai 1989). Persons and groups were now increasingly seen to 'migrate, regroup in new locations, reconstruct their histories, and refigure their ethnic "projects"' (Appadurai 1991:191). These programmatic calls stimulated new approaches to the study of diasporas and transnational communities. More precisely, they recommended that this research be designed to focus on movement 'as a lens through which to examine the supposedly normal condition of being attached to a territorialised polity and an identifiable people' (Malkki 1995a:516).

Such an agenda raises the question of how concepts of 'home' and 'homeland' are fashioned in parts of Southeast Asia that are marked by continued nation-making, alongside cultures of migrancy emerging as prior forms of mobility are reworked for modern times. The challenge posed for speakers at the 25th Annual Indonesia Lecture Series was to open up the issue of how 'horizons' of home—spatial, temporal and political—are delineated and experienced in contemporary island Southeast Asia. Connections and patterns of mobility in Southeast Asia precede and thus pay little heed to the borders of the postcolonial nation-states that nowadays describe the region. While the theme 'horizons of home', therefore, demanded some broadening of the usual ethnographic frame of reference for the lecture series, this volume remains exploratory, with no attempt at a comprehensive coverage of island Southeast Asia.[1]

Of the eight papers that comprise the volume, some were initially presented on the occasion of the 25th Annual Indonesia Lecture Series and others were added later for the particular perspective they bring to the theme. In good eastern Indonesian style, the papers in this volume can also be read as a series of complementary pairs, with each pair providing a closer comparative focus on a particular aspect of the theme.

The first pair focuses on the pivotal role of ideas of 'homeland' in two distinctly different forms of contemporary nation-making. Sara Graham analyses Xanana Gusmão's deploying of the once-derogatory term *maubere* in his creation of a compelling discourse on 'the sacred and beloved homeland' during the long struggle for East Timor (Ramos-Horta 1987:37; Gusmão 2000a; 2000b). This discourse and Graham's reading of it are especially interesting in the light of Benedict Anderson's posing of the question of what made it possible to 'think East Timor' (1993:24). His well-known theoretical model of 'the origins of national consciousness' (Anderson 1983) focuses on the spread of print and its relationship to capitalism, whereas in this case the model comes up against an East Timor in which there was very little capitalism and illiteracy was widespread.

In lieu of print-capitalism, Anderson (1993:27) noted the profoundly nationalising effects of the colonial relationship that Indonesia instituted with East Timor after its invasion in 1975: the expansion of the state meant schools and development projects and also the Indonesian requirement that its citizens follow one of the officially sanctioned religions. Thus, consciousness of being 'East Timorese' spread rapidly as more of the ethnically and linguistically diverse population became Catholics, both for protection and as an expression of common suffering, and the local Church hierarchy's decision to use Tetun established a language of religion and identity. Anderson (1993:26) also suggests that Indonesian military leaders failed to see how this colonial relationship replayed, in reverse, Indonesia's own independence struggle against the Dutch during which the nationalist movement was shaped by Indonesia's Dutch-educated elite. In 1986, as a few thousand young East Timorese studied in Indonesian universities in a social environment that demanded 'gratitude', they received a lengthy message from Xanana Gusmão.[2] In this volume, Sara Graham analyses the message to see how it constructs the homeland rhetorically as an object of moral obligation and a sacred imperative for resistance fighters and educated youth alike.

As East Timorese outside the territory were exhorted to be willing to make the ultimate sacrifice for their homeland, so Filipinos overseas are encouraged to show their loyalty by being 'great workers' and 'global ambassadors' for the Philippines. Claire Kelly's paper discusses this emerging global Filipino nation. While she treats all the main categories of Filipinos overseas as transmigrants (including permanent residents, contract workers, undocumented workers and visa overstayers), she focuses on the migrant workers who must endure commodification on the global market and marginalisation in the host country. To cope, some join grassroots organisations abroad that require adherence to strict rules about public behaviour and friendships so as to represent their identities as morally responsible women serving church, family, community and country of origin (Chang & Groves 2000). Some gain a sense of community via the pages of domestic-worker magazines, or on internet sites where they share their narratives of homeland and identity. The question that Kelly poses is whether these spaces reinforce an idealised form of national identity, or enable challenges to such hegemonic constructions. She notes that neither the magazines, nor the virtual communities offer critical insight into the politics of migrant labour, although online forums that foster identification with the global community enable Filipinos worldwide to discuss and debate shared concerns.

What her analysis reveals is that 'Filipino nationalist discourse is itself transnational and that it is often migrants as well as government agents who take up this discourse'. Thus, domestic-worker magazines represent an ethics of familialism and economic duty, the online communities promote selected aspects of Filipino-ness and the state deploys tropes that emphasise national allegiance and national identity. Kelly concludes that Filipino transmigrants are thereby 'subjected to discipline by the nation-state, the capitalist workplace (for domestic workers, the household) and the diasporic community itself'. If, as Hage (1993:76), developing Bauman's (1992) view of nationalism, argues, 'To be a national is to "possess" a territory, without which there is no national existence', Kelly's paper suggests that this is no less true of transnational Filipinos, who may be living outside the territory but are nonetheless subjects of the discursive practices of the home state.

The next pair of papers focuses on the movement of Indonesian nationals both within and beyond their homeland. Graeme Hugo notes that Indonesians are currently 'more mobile and range over a wider area...than ever before'. In an exemplary analysis, he points out the limitations in the available demographic data and the research on causes and consequences of migration, as he analyses Indonesian population mobility to identify changes in patterns of migration and the major issues associated with these changes. Internal migration, he finds, is characterised by the strong representation of young adults and better-educated groups; rural to urban migration in which men outnumber women over long distances but women predominate in short-distance moves to cities; and female migrants who are concentrated in factory work, domestic work and the sex/ entertainment sector. Hugo stresses that statistics on internal migration fail to detect most non-permanent circular migration, long significant in Indonesia and showing a massive increase 'in scale, complexity and importance in recent years'. This circular migration, in which people from rural areas find work in the urban informal sector, leaving their families behind, is, he argues, of greater significance in most parts of Indonesia than permanent migration.

Such circulation prefigures the international labour migration that Hugo shows has grown substantially since the 1990s. While the Indonesian government has reason to encourage international labour migration, Hugo notes that exploitation of workers occurs at all stages of the process. He traces the shift to Asian destinations for official migrants and the major routes that undocumented migrants take to Malaysia, where sectors of the economy (construction, plantations, domestic workers, forestry) are so heavily reliant on Indonesian labour that they 'may not be viable without access to that labour'. In analysing how the origins of migrant workers are strongly geographically concentrated in parts of West Java and eastern Indonesia, Hugo highlights how the impact of migration is magnified in those areas. Thus, remittances sent home from Malaysia to families in West Nusa Tenggara have been known to exceed the entire provincial budget. In conclusion, Hugo suggests that the migration industry and civil society face challenges in training and protecting migrant workers, as he identifies a series of 'drivers' that he expects will continue to stimulate the scale and complexity of Indonesian migration and circulation into the future.

Emigration from Indonesia is increasing. Graeme Hugo notes in his paper that the Indonesian-born community in Australia grew rapidly between 1996 and 2003. In considering 'Indonesians as Australians', Janet Penny's paper builds on her doctoral research for which she interviewed 100 Indonesians who had migrated to Australia between 1947 and 1986. She also draws on subsequent research that included some Indonesian-Australian families in a comparative project on intermarriage as a context of migration and integration. Here she reflects on issues in her informants' lives that shed light on the intersection of their cultural values with the changing national contexts that have shaped the experience of different streams of Indonesian migrants to Australia. Indonesians, she notes, have always lived in a multi-cultural society and most of those she interviewed had previous experience of mobility and adaptation. At the same time, adaptation did not preclude the maintenance of an Indonesian identity, as 'those who had moved most' were not only 'those who used English most' but also 'the most active participants in Indonesian cultural activities'. Of the six migrant groups (American, Dutch, Italian, Lebanese Indonesian, Chinese) in the 1996 *Intermarriage* study, the Indonesian participants were found to be the most likely to consciously choose and to succeed in a strategy to 'combine the values and behaviour of both cultures'.

Religious affiliation is clearly reflected in Janet Penny's data on the attraction of Indonesian migrants to Australia: in 1986, while only 9% of Indonesia's population was Christian, in Australia 42% of ethnic Indonesians and 67% of ethnic Chinese-Indonesians were Christians. At the same time, while 87% of Indonesia's population were Muslims, only 43% of ethnic Indonesians living in Australia were Muslims. These figures call for research on the experiences of living in Australia of Indonesians of diverse cultural backgrounds and religious orientations.[3] Apart from religion, Indonesians in Australia report needing to negotiate contrasting values in relation to social harmony, social hierarchy, and participation in support networks.

As Janet Penny outlines, the historical and political contexts for the negotiation of Indonesian migrant identities have varied considerably from the Australia of the 1940s through to the present time. This is reflected in the plans and changes of mind that she reports, and the complex trajectories for home-making and sense of belonging. In seeking correlates for long-term commitment to staying in Australia, she considers a number of variables: ethnicity, education, socio-economic status, time spent planning the move and motives for the move. Patterns of commitment, she finds, tend to be influenced by the circumstances of the move. Discussing migrants' future plans, she notes, 'Homes are provisional, implying a strong sense of loss alongside the sense of gain when a new home has been chosen'.

The following pair of papers takes up issues of loss, displacement and emplacement with respect to the historical migration of two of the main maritime peoples of archipelagic Southeast Asia. Phillip Winn's illuminating paper discusses the ways Butonese long-settled in the Banda Islands regard their ancestral homeland of Buton. The Dutch East India Company took control of the Banda Islands, a major source of nutmeg and mace, in 1621 and set in train two population movements: the expulsion of nearly the entire population of 13,000–15,000 people and their replacement by other incoming peoples over several centuries. The newcomers included 'slaves, convicts, indentured or contract ("coolie") labour and freely arriving in-migrants'. Winn's paper focuses on those contemporary inhabitants of the Bandas (20–30% of the population in 1999) who acknowledge ancestral origins in the Tukang Besi Islands and are thus known as Butonese. The Tukang Besi Islands, renowned for out-migration, have played a prominent part in the characterisation of the Butonese as one of the most mobile populations in eastern Indonesia. But as the term 'Butonese' embraces 14 different languages and more than a dozen islands, Winn makes a compelling case that the category highlights why we need to reject bounded notions of ethnic identity based on shared language and territory, in favour of examining instead the more dynamic, situational and often strategic dimensions of particular contexts of identification.

In this vein, Winn describes the Butonese of the Banda Islands as differentiated into two segments. These are marked by the pace of change in language shift and naming styles, as well as differences in discourses on the status of ancestors and the Buton sultanate. One segment consists of those who descend predominantly from nutmeg plantation labourers and live in old, mixed settlements of Butonese and non-Butonese. The other segment is comprised of 'those associated with concentrated settlements of Butonese or enclaves that had developed on the periphery of the plantation system'. People from these enclave settlements are much more likely to link their identity with the Buton sultanate and envision their in-migrating ancestors as high-status figures who left Buton in 'an active quest for good fortune'. In contrast, the migration narratives of those descended from plantation labourers depict their ancestors as being of low status, and fleeing a Buton where the authority of the sultan and the demands of corvee labour were harsh. In these latter accounts, the Banda Islands are valorised as more socially egalitarian than homeland Buton, a trait that is considered especially fitting for a community of Muslims. In Winn's analysis, these contrasting visions of the ancestral homeland are linked to varying levels of adherence to Butonese traditions in the Bandas and the extent to which some Butonese are more disposed to embrace the local practices of the Banda islands. This paper therefore highlights how distinct social constructions of the homeland and the grounds of ancestral displacement continue to inflect long-settled descendants' approaches to emplacement elsewhere.

If Butonese ancestors went to the Bandas seeking refuge, even more than good fortune, Riwanto Tirtosudarmo's paper presents Buginese migration across the Makassar Strait from Sulawesi to the east coast of Borneo as a model of expanding influence. He notes that traders from Wajo' were already established in east Borneo by the early 18th century, when they were joined by a Bugis prince who concluded 'political matrimonial alliances with local rulers' and organised Wajo' communities all down the coast 'each under its elected chiefs' (Pelras 1996:321). This migration from Wajo' to East Kalimantan continued and, within the Republic of Indonesia, was stimulated by the Kahar Muzakkar rebellion (1950–65), improvements in shipping during the 1970s and a flow of 'new migrants' in the 1980s. The 'old Bugis', regarded as descendants of those who first settled in the area, mostly reside in Samarinda-Seberang, on the south bank of the Mahakam River, in the city that lends its name to the Bugis textile produced there, *sarong* Samarinda. As permanent migration gives way to emerging patterns of circulation for Bugis traders and weavers alike, Tirtosudarmo raises the interpretive possibility that 'population mobility has removed administrative and geographic boundaries between provinces'. In his view, the ease of movement across the Strait now makes the Bugis settlement at Samarinda-Seberang a 'home away from home' that is slowly being integrated into a larger Bugis cultural domain.

Citing Bugis dominance in the bureaucracy and economic sectors, particularly trade and transportation, Tirtosudarmo turns to the issue of ethnic relations and potential for conflict. In the identity politics of East Kalimantan, Dayak and Kutai (Malay) are regarded as 'indigenous', while Javanese, Buginese and Banjarese are 'migrants'. A revitalisation of Dayak identity has occurred here, as elsewhere in Kalimantan, in the context of depletion of natural resources and 'growing competition between ethnic groups'. Dayak identity appears in the local response to the regional autonomy laws (passed in 1999 and revised in 2004). On Tirtosudarmo's analysis, the discourse of local leaders, demanding a separate province in the north of East Kalimantan to 'accelerate development' there, can be seen as an expression of ethnic-indigenous based demands to be 'recognised as the owner of the region and its resources'. As Tambiah (1996:130) has noted, such situations can become particularly acrimonious,

> when power shifts to and is exercised by the most numerous, usually the local 'sons of the soil', who then wish to displace…successful migrants…viewed as obstacles to the social mobility and well-being of the indigenous majority.

Resentment towards 'migrants' in East Kalimantan has not, however, erupted into violent conflicts of the kind witnessed in recent times in other parts of Kalimantan (Peluso 2006; ICG 2001a; 2001b).[4] This relative peace, Tirtosudarmo suggests, may reflect two factors: first, the difficulty of mobilising Dayak resentment into a wider movement, as their number is proportionally small (fewer than 10% in year 2000) and their settlements are concentrated in the hinterland, mostly in the northern part of the province; and second, the very success of the Bugis who have not only 'penetrated the local economy and political structure', but also 'contributed significantly to establishing a new multi-ethnic society strongly dominated by Bugis culture'. Nonetheless, Tirtosudarmo's paper shows that an 'indigenous' challenge based in a minority segment of the population may have to be indirect and draw on alternative discourses like 'development' when seeking to escape the dominance achieved by Bugis migrants who have so successfully 'emplaced' themselves in east Borneo.

The final pair of papers considers ideas of 'home' and 'homeland' in the context of identity, migrancy and gender relations. Eric Hobsbawm (1991) has pointed out the contradiction inherent in two senses of 'home' that he distinguishes in German as the 'essentially private' *heim*: a roof over one's head, remembered in the concrete sense of household, family, face-to-face relations; and the 'essentially public' *heimat*: a place of origin—a city, country, province, land—more a social construction than a real memory and conceived of as a public universe. At the limit, he suggests, this latter becomes the imagined community of the nation (*Heimatland, Vaterland*). It seems that the Germanic *heim* derives from Indo-European *kei*, 'implying lying down, a bed or couch, and something dear or beloved', so suggesting a place to lay your head (Hollander 1991:44). The English 'home' derives from the Anglo-Saxon word *ham*, 'a village or town, an estate or possession', a meaning later consolidated between the 17th and 19th centuries in English case law and popular imagination as implying 'a haven which comprises both house and surrounding land' (Hollander 1991:44; Rykwert 1991:53; Mallett 2004:65). In the Lamaholot language of eastern Flores, Indonesia, the dyadic expression *léwo tana* refers to a ritually constituted community and its land. In my chapter in this volume, I discuss the significance of land as a productive resource in Lamaholot communities, analysing gender relations and associated constraints on access to land as factors that impact on whether women labour in the fields at home or journey to work abroad.

Cynthia Enloe (2000:44) famously declared that 'nationalism typically has sprung from masculinised memory, masculinised humiliation and masculinised hope', pointing out how women's experiences are submerged in anti-colonial nationalisms. Discussing nationalism and gender relations, Nira Yuval-Davis (2001:128) notes that women come to represent the homeland, as well as the home. She argues that gender relations are crucial to the construction of 'home' as a site for the constitution of ways of life to be passed on from generation to generation. Furthermore, the close association between collective territory, collective identity and womanhood means that women are seen as 'the embodiment of the homeland', the symbolic bearers of the collectivity's identity and honour (Yuval-Davis 2001:126–8). Taking issue with the focus on cultural and symbolic dimensions of women's participation in ethnic or national projects, Sylvia Walby (1996:242) calls for more attention to the economic and the sexual division of labour in this context. She emphasises women's differential involvement in ethnic or national projects, arguing that women's political activities tend to be either more globally or locally focused than those of men and less nationalist (Walby 1996:244–52). For diasporic communities, Yuval-Davis notes that the homeland has become the site of young men's search for brides. For the people of Flores, the opposite is the case. With so many men travelling to work in Malaysia, it is 'widows' left behind and young unmarried women who set out from home literally in search of their menfolk abroad.

Ideas of staying, leaving and journeying are all integrally associated with notions of 'home' and are, in turn, linked to ideas of dependency, independence and autonomy. Journeys away from home are thought to constitute home and traveller, establishing the 'thresholds and boundaries of home', particularly associated with the experience of 'being at home'. For some authors, 'being at home' can be a matter of affect or feeling—the presence or absence of particular feelings—a state of being that is not necessarily bounded by a physical location (Mallett 2004:77–9). For others, 'a sense of home is grounded less in a place per se than in the activity that goes on in a place' (Jackson 1995:148). In the final paper in this volume, Catharina Purwani Williams explores some of these aspects of 'home' as she traces the shifting subjectivity of female migrants from eastern Indonesia as they travel to work in the urban centres of Surabaya and Makassar. During her research for a larger study (Williams 2007), she conducted interviews with 15 women in caring professions (seven teachers and eight nurses), whom she sees adopting these 'feminised occupations' as a means of breaking free of 'the confines of gendered expectation at home'. She emphasises the women's agency in leaving home to achieve their personal goals of greater autonomy and independence. On Williams' analysis, the women find in their migration, 'a space to manoeuvre within the interplay of local gender relations and the dominant femininity'. Once they gained mobility, she suggests, the women were 'on the path toward new possibilities' as migration allowed them to explore a sense of self and was 'a significant step in creating a space to feel at home'.

Since the 25th Annual Indonesia Lecture Series, the ideas of 'home' and 'homeland' have taken on particularly evocative and instrumental meanings in the discourses on 'home-grown terrorism' and 'homeland security'. These inflections conflate the intimacies of 'home' with the threat of terror from and/ or within the nation, so summoning the state to its defence. In the aftermath of 11 September 2001, Pnina Werbner (2004:451–2) wrote of what she calls the 'vulnerability' of diasporas,

> – the process whereby global events can precipitate radical diasporic estrangement...fed by public moral panics surrounding the danger of Islamic 'terror' or 'disloyalty', expressed in the speeches of politicians, newspapers columns, and global news reports.

Speaking of British South Asian Muslims, she posed the question: 'What must it be like to feel under siege in one's own home?' For some diaspora communities, she notes, this is a recurring experience, as a history of repeated expulsions has led to a cycle of persecution, exile and peaceful sojourning in a continuing 'alternation between alienation and consolidation' (Werbner 2004:469). In her view, this raises the wider issue of 'whether members of diaspora communities can ever fully cease to be strangers' (Werbner 2004:468-9). Winn's discussion (this volume) of the notion of diaspora and its current prominence as an analytical term applied to diverse socio-cultural contexts, similarly highlights how diasporic groups are marked not only by nostalgia for the homeland, but also by 'a feeling of provisionality or ambivalence at the host location'.

If a history of repeated expulsions has led some diasporic groups to oscillate between experiences of provisional emplacement and further alienation, always tinged with nostalgia for the original homeland, this may form the limit case for the concept of 'displacement'. Fox (2001:67) defines displacement not merely as 'the movement or transference of populations', but more specifically as 'the processes of establishing locations or "placements" for such populations in which an attachment to some former place is retained as a critical feature of identity'. While displacement always begins with a departure, Fox insists it is more than 'the social creation of place in a new location'. The key feature of displacement is that

> the departure itself may affect—temper, inform and possibly determine—the new placement. Thus, displacement can be dynamic, creative, reactive, adjustive, but its defining quality is the nature of the remembrance embodied in the act of creation of place and retention of that remembrance (Fox 2001:67).

In this vein, Winn's chapter in this volume shows how the differential rank and circumstances of ancestors departing Buton continue to inform the nature of their long-settled descendants' remembrance of homeland and, as a result, practices of attachment to the Banda Islands. In his broader theoretical reflection, Winn compares the notion of diaspora with the Malay-Indonesian discourse of *merantau*, contrasting the nostalgia and ambivalence of the perpetually displaced that attaches to diaspora with the capacity for agency and 'the possibility of profound (re)connection with new locations' that inheres in *merantau*. He concludes that the discourse of *merantau* is thus better suited than notions of diaspora to capturing the multiple meanings of 'departure', as these give rise not only to displacement, but also to re-emplacement. I would add that island Southeast Asia is a rich source of discourses of departure. As well as the Malay-Indonesian *merantau*, there is the Ibanic discourse of *bejalai*, that in Borneo encodes a similar set of meanings, as in 'to go on a journey with the intention of acquiring material profit and social prestige' (Kedit 1980:235). But there are also parallel discourses offering alternative interpretations. Thus, in eastern Flores, common use of the discourse of *merantau* does not preclude local challenges to that notion as being far too grandiose for what Florenese achieve in journeying to Sabah: 'We do not really *merantau*', I was told, 'what we do is *melarat*'.[5] This statement, clearly voicing a critique, was explained to me as meaning that far from attaining good fortune overseas, men from Flores who go abroad tend to roam and wander like nomads and vagabonds (*mengembara*). Be that as it may, such parallel discourses and local critiques provide a comparative context for considering the adequacy of analytical concepts and the assumptions these encode. Winn is making the point that local discourses must be analysed for more than their implication in the ethnographic account. As he notes, terms designating population movements, like *pengungsi* or 'refugee', will have evolving social meanings that must be traced. And a localised discourse like *merantau*, free of the presumption of ethnic homogeneity that has bedevilled our analytical concepts, should be considered 'a potentially useful means of escaping the limitations of our own intervening assumptions'. This is an important insight from island Southeast Asia.

As Hage (1993:102) has noted of another time and place 'even nomads mourn their home' and yearn to find another. Together the papers in this volume contribute to developing an understanding of how 'horizons of home'—spatial, temporal and political—inflect home-making in the present and describe social processes of departure, displacement and emplacement in contemporary island Southeast Asia.

Endnotes

1   I would like to thank the Monash Asia Institute for supporting the Lecture Series
     and the MAI Publications Officers, Emma Hegarty and Jenny Hall, for their work
     on the production of this volume.

2   Interestingly, Gusmão composed the message in Portuguese with the heading
     Mensagem aos jovens catolicos de Timor Leste, estudando na Indonesia [Message
     to the Catholic youth of East Timor, students in Indonesia]. The text was entitled
     Uma historia que pulsa na alma maubere [A history that beats in the *maubere*
     soul] for publication in Portuguese in 1994 in *Timor Leste: um povo, uma pátria*,
     Edições Colibri, Lisbon. The English translation published by Sarah Niner was
     prepared in association with East Timorese colleagues (for details, see Niner
     2000a). Portuguese, the language in which Gusmão expressed himself best at
     this time, was the semi-official language of communication for the East Timorese
     resistance. It enabled some degree of secrecy should materials fall into the wrong
     hands. Messages like this would be circulated within the clandestine movement,
     sometimes in written format, but often on cassette tapes, as cassettes were
     easier for East Timorese to duplicate without detection (Sarah Niner, personal
     communication, 14 May 2008).

3   A number of such studies are currently underway, including those by Dr Dewi
     Jayanti (Balinese in Australia), Dr Suparto (Muslim Indonesians in Australia) and
     Monika Winarnita Doxey (Indonesian Australian cross-cultural families).

4   The conflicts in West and Central Kalimantan between Dayaks and Madurese
     migrants, whom Dayaks see as having dispossessed them of land and economic
     opportunities, have left a combined death toll in outbreaks since 1999 of well over
     1,000 and number of displaced people close to 100,000 (see ICG 2005).

5   Echols and Shadily (1997:330,367) list two meanings, both deriving from *larat*,
     for *melarat* 1, 'poor, miserable' (hence *melaratkan* 'impoverish, make poor
     and miserable') and 2, *melarat* protracted (illness, etc) from *larat* meaning i,
     be protracted, be drawn out; ii, drag (of anchor); iii, wander. Poerwadarminta
     (1976:568,641) also lists two meanings for *melarat* 1, i, '*rugi*; *kerugian*;' ii, '*miskin*;
     sengsara;' and 2, from *larat* meaning '*hanyut*; *pergi jauh-jauh*; *makin bertambah
     jauh (luas, lama, panjang, sangat dsb)*;' as in, for example, '*larat ke negri orang*'
     meaning '*pergi ke negri orang (mencari penghidupan)*' and '*orang larat*' meaning
     '*orang yang mengembara*', yielding the forms *berlarat(-larat)* and *melarat* as in,
     for example, *berlarat-larat ke seberang lautan*.

The sacred and beloved *maubere* homeland: home, nation and resistance in East Timor

Sara Graham

High on the mountain peaks of Timor
The grass grows
And warms the fractured bones
Of a fighter who fell
Down on the grassy plains of Timor
A flower shows
And beautifies the bones
Of a fighter who fell

(Xanana Gusmão, in Tippet 1999)

The fallen fighter has become a central motif in East Timorese nationalist imaginings. He (for the resistance fighter is most often male) epitomises what it means to be *maubere* (Gusmão 2000a:35) . To call oneself *maubere* is to identify not simply as East Timorese,[1] but with a politics and national yearning and to claim a particular place in the East Timorese struggle for the *maubere* homeland. Fretilin's appropriation of *maubere* brought it into current usage in East Timor, transforming it from a racial epithet into a symbol of national pride (Arenas 1999:3). Fretilin leaders reclaimed *maubere*, a Mambai[2] expression of brotherhood used derogatively by the Portuguese, to symbolically link the disparate East Timorese ethno-linguistic groups, creating a nexus between the *maubere* and the land. However, the term has a symbolic meaning that runs much deeper than this in the context of resistance to Indonesian colonialism and oppression. For East Timorese nationalists, to be *maubere* means to make a choice between 'Homeland or Death' (Gusmão 2000b:101). It means making a choice to sacrifice one's life, if necessary, for the survival of the *maubere* nation.

This chapter is based upon my analysis of a message composed by Xanana Gusmão in May 1986 and addressed to educated East Timorese youth. In the message Gusmão outlines the political and cultural basis of the resistance, calling upon the youth of East Timor to carry on the struggle of their forebears for the liberation of their homeland from Indonesian occupation. The document raises questions of acquiescence to offers of autonomy within an Indonesian state and concerns about the physical and cultural survival of the *maubere* people. I examine the rhetorical devices through which homeland is employed

15

as a symbol of nation to stir people to fight, to endure, and to die for their nation.

Gusmão's message provides a succinct illustration of the use of historical and symbolic devices in the nationalist discourse of the East Timorese resistance. Homeland is a central theme throughout the document, providing a cogent piece of writing for an analysis of the role of 'homeland' as a potent symbol in *maubere* nationalism. It was written within two months of the formation of a coalition between Fretilin and UDT and is a rallying cry for broader participation in the East Timorese struggle for independence.

The message has approximately 20,000 words. It is divided into four sections: 'Autonomy or independence?'; 'Homeland or death!'; 'End of the conflict'; and 'The position of the Church in East Timor'. These sections reflect the political realities that precipitated serious reconsideration of the path the nationalist struggle would take at the time of writing. I have chosen not to provide a linear analysis of Gusmão's message using his four major sub-headings. Instead I have drawn upon themes that permeate the message in providing a statement of national intent, rallying East Timorese youth to the *maubere* nationalist cause. The remainder of my chapter is divided into four parts:

- 'A history that beats in the *maubere* soul' examines the role of history in invigorating *maubere* nationalism;

- 'Sacred and beloved homeland' interrogates the construction of homeland as a central motif in *maubere* nationalism which naturalises the nation, removing it from politics and delivering it into the realm of the sacred;

- 'Beloved youth and *maubere* patriots' explores the role of young East Timorese in the resistance;

- 'Homeland or death' draws upon themes illuminated in my previous three sections to illustrate the intimate connection between homeland and national survival.

A history that beats in the *maubere* soul

Maubere nationalism is oriented toward the future, toward self determination and toward a place in the modern international community of nation-states. Yet it imbeds itself in history or, more specifically, a *maubere* history built on bloody sacrifice and resistance against foreign domination. Gusmão (2000b:92) says: 'It is a history that beats in the *Maubere* soul that guides our actions… For us, Beloved Youth and *Maubere* Patriots, our history belongs to our own people and it is our own people who make our history'. This view echoes the sentiment of Bengali nationalist Bankimchandra Chattopadhyay, a 19th century Indian intellectual whose claim 'we must have a history' (Chatterjee 1993:75) was a call for the power of self-representation. Katherine Verdery (1996:227) argues that a common culture and history are crucial to the development of nationalisms. Nationalists draw upon history to engender a sense of national belonging and identification with national aspirations.

This culture and history need not, however, be homogenous to have discursive power. The geographical territory of East Timor is inhabited by a diverse range of ethno-linguistic groups, as well as *assimilados, mestiços, deportados* and their descendants, whose varied cultural heritage is joined in a common colonial history. No doubt the impact of Portuguese colonialism upon the urban-dwelling Catholic, Portuguese-speaking *assimilado* was radically different from its impact on the rural villager from whom *corvée* was extracted. Despite this, the common experience of oppression under the colonial regime has been a leitmotif in the nationalist struggle and has united diverse groups with different experiences of oppression. It could be suggested that a varied culture and history, which allows a diverse range of groups to attach meaning to the national symbols that arise through expression of culture, facilitates peoples' ownership of the national symbols and, by extension, generates a greater stake in the nation and therefore a greater stake in fighting and dying for national survival.

Gusmão suggests that the people of the territory now known as East Timor have never acquiesced to domination by foreign powers. He writes:

> The history of our people was made with life and blood sacrifices by our people repudiating foreign domination...the history of the people of East Timor is a history of blood, of weakness, of difficulties, of civil resistance! The people of East Timor continue today to determine the course of their own history with the words of their own historical existence written in their blood (Gusmão 2000b:92).

On this view, local groups in East Timor have rebelled against successive waves of foreign domination in what Geoffrey Gunn (2000a) has termed the '500 year *funu*'.[3] They have staged uprisings against Portuguese colonialism, struggled against the brief Japanese occupation during the Second World War and maintained a protracted resistance against the 25-year Indonesian occupation.

Timorese school teachers of nationalist persuasion taught about historical figures who were in some way anti-colonial, such as the Timorese Dom Boaventura and the Indonesian Raden Adjeng Kartini. Dom Boaventura, a powerful *luriai* (chief), united many ethno-linguistic groups of the territory to wage a 17-year rebellion against the Portuguese, culminating in an uprising and eventual defeat in 1912. He is considered by many to be the first East Timorese nationalist fighter (Dunn 1996:17; Taylor 1999:11; Ramos-Horta 1987:19). The ASDT leaders were anxious to establish themselves as heirs to Dom Boaventura's legacy of anti-colonial rebellion, and were aided by the membership of his widow, Queen Maria, in the association (Hill 1978:85). Kartini, a member of the Javanese aristocracy at the turn of the 20th century, campaigned for the emancipation of women through education. She also criticised Dutch colonial rule and is honoured by Indonesians as a national heroine (Jayawardena 1986:145). Although not directly connected with the struggle against Indonesia, such figures have inspired young East Timorese to involve themselves in the resistance (Arenas 1998:14). Furthermore, the figure of Kartini, a reminder of Indonesia's own protracted struggle against foreign domination, provides a potent illustration of the hypocrisy of the Indonesian occupation of East Timor. Rebellion against colonialism has become part of the East Timorese collective memory, the freedom fighter a dominant trope in *maubere* identity and resistance a defining characteristic of the '*maubere* soul'.

Sacred and beloved homeland

MAUBERE People,
MAUBERE, child of East Timor,
tear open your belly,
your cravings,
ruts of neglect, of anguish, of oppression,
and hurl them to the wind,
to your furthest brother
in the secret places of the sacred land
of your parents, of your children,
of your grandparents, of your grandchildren ...

(*Maubere*, by Xanana Gusmão 2000a:35)

The sacred land of the *maubere*, the children of Timor, is the land of one's parents and children, one's grandparents and grandchildren. In Gusmão's writing the familial ties reach back into the past and are projected into the future, yet are grounded in the present through familial connections to brothers that stretch out to the farthest secret reaches of the land. Here the *maubere* nation is imagined as a national family, homeland is fundamental to the construction of the *maubere* nation. Home is a prominent metaphor in nationalist thought (Hage 1993:79). The Latin root of 'nation' is *natio,* meaning 'birth, to be born'. This places the nation, as a category, in the domestic realm of home and family. Nationalism is often imagined in familial terms: the motherland, the fatherland, blood and kin (Anderson 1983; McClintock 1993:63; Pettman 1996:45). Affective terminology masks the political nature of nationalism by naturalising the relationships between the constituents of the nation, symbolically removing the nation from politics and projecting it into the realm of the sacred (McClintock 1993:63; Verdery 1996:226). In this section, I analyse the construction of East Timor as the homeland of the *Timor Oan* (Children of Timor). I illustrate the nexus between familial imaginings of the nation figured as natural and the image of the sacred nation that transcends politics. I argue that the discourse of homeland is not merely symbolic. It acts materially to naturalise both the politics of the nation and the relationships between members of the nation. In turn it naturalises the moral imperative compelling the *Timor Oan* to fight and die for the sacred *maubere* homeland.

Home represents warmth, safety and succour. Home is also the site of domestication. It is in the home that children are initiated into the cultural practices and understandings of the family which they are expected to adopt as their own. Children thus amass a coded set of cultural understandings that provide a prism through which they can make sense of the wider world and their place within it. The coded nature of familial interaction means that home is also a private space. Only the initiated have intimate access to and an understanding of the nuances of familial relationships. Home therefore provides a safe space, closed to the intrusion of outsiders. Hage (1993:79) suggests 'home, nation and family operate within the same mythic metaphorical field' to offer 'familiarity and security'. The nation is commonly imagined as a home, a secure and unified space of return that offers protection from external threat. Similarly the national home is a place of belonging. According to Michael Ignatieff (1993:10), nationalists claim that full belonging, based upon a deep identification with the coded cultural understandings of the homeland, is only possible among one's own people in one's own native land.

Home is projected as a source of love. For *maubere* nationalists the native land of the *maubere* is not simply a homeland, it is a 'beloved Homeland' (Gusmão 2000b). The love of nation is likened to a familial love, both a source of protection from external threat and itself in need of protection. It is the love of homeland that inspires 'Beloved Youth' to become '*Maubere* Patriots' (Gusmão 2000b). The resistance of the 'thousand-times heroic people of East Timor' (Gusmão 2000b:104) against the oppressive Indonesian occupation is sustained by a love of homeland. Domestic love is symbolised as political love. The homeland becomes the source of love as one loves a mother, father, sister or brother (Elshtain 1993:169). The love of homeland finds its greatest expression through opposition to intruders. If, as the Indonesian generals anticipated, the East Timorese resistance had collapsed and the population acquiesced to East Timor's continued occupation, the East Timorese population may not have suffered the same degree of brutality as they did over 25 years. However, the love of homeland and all that it represents, security, identity, belonging, and ultimately freedom, was a powerful force motivating continued struggle in the face of a ruthless invading military regime.

As love of the homeland compels one to protect the nation from external aggressors, the nation, the source of protection and succour, finds itself intimately connected with death. Blood is a recurring metaphor in the *maubere* nationalist struggle. The history of the *maubere* is a history 'written in their blood' (Gusmão 2000b:92). The *maubere* conscience runs in *maubere* blood (Gusmão 2000b:107). Sacrifice is 'blood sacrifice' (Gusmão 2000b:92), the homeland despoiled by 'rivers of blood' (Gusmão 2000b:89). For the resistance blood symbolises life and death, hope and despair, continuity and loss. Blood is the fluid that sustains life. Its transmission through the generations, through the 'Beloved Youth', ensures national continuity. Through the connection to life and death, blood attains its emotional power as a metaphor in nationalist thought. It is through the patriotic actions of *maubere* youth that blood symbolises life, hope and continuity, its spillage death, despair and loss.

Blood symbolises familial connection, transmitted through the generations. It is also employed as a metaphor for the ties that bind the homeland. The homeland is projected as a place of belonging for those of the same blood. Gusmão illustrates the use of this metaphor succinctly when he writes: 'The Falintil guerrillas, your blood brothers and children of the same Homeland, prefer to die fighting…rather than to betray, and vilify the blood that covers this sacred and beloved Homeland' (2000b:94). The *maubere* nation is conceived of as a family in which all members are connected by blood. This connection impels loyalty to the *maubere* nation. Brotherhood implies equality.[4] The blood of one brother is of no lesser or greater inherent value than the blood of another. If one's blood brother, a Falintil guerrilla, is prepared to spill his blood for the nation it would be a betrayal of fraternal loyalty not to be similarly prepared to fight and die.

However, this usage contains an interesting paradox. Gusmão needs to draw to the attention of the youth he is addressing that Falintil guerrillas are their blood brothers. The relationship between siblings is usually intimate, emotive and self evident. There is little need to spell out the connection. Siblings implicitly understand their place in the familial order and their connections to one another. In the nation, however, connections are neither self evident nor intimate. As Anderson (1983:15) remarks, members of a nation will never meet the majority of other members. He argues that the connection is an imagined one. Gusmão, through his use of the metaphor of the blood brother, is asking his audience to imagine themselves as active members of the 'sacred and beloved Homeland' (2000b:94) of the Falintil guerrillas. He requires them to be prepared to spill their blood in an act of fraternal solidarity in defence of the *maubere* nation.

In nationalist thought blood is precious. It invigorates the continued struggle for nation. Gusmão (2000b:104) states,

> it is only through total confidence in the strength of our people irrigated by their own blood, strengthened and fertilised by fallen bodies and with an always-renewing faith that we can (if we put all our shoulders to the wheel) guarantee our people the realisation of their objective: securing our own historical identity.

On this reading the fallen fighter makes the land bountiful, providing promise for the future of the struggle. Blood fuels the struggle as it fuels the body. The spilled blood of the fallen fighter at once engenders despair as it ignites hope. It is the despair of the loss of a beloved brother or sister and the hope that is distilled in the slogan 'to resist is to win' (Gusmão 2000b:126). If continued resistance is viewed by *maubere* nationalists as the path to national liberation, if resistance itself is a victory over oppression, the fallen fighter is a symbol of the determination of the true *maubere* patriot never to give up the struggle. They assert that the struggle cannot be lost as long as there are patriots willing to fight to the last. In the words of an independence supporter prior to the Popular Consultation[5] in 1999: 'We will fight for our homeland until there is no-one left. If only one person is left standing to govern our homeland then we have won' (*Scenes from an occupation* 1999). Gusmão (2000b:88) states that '[t]he armed resistance...expresses the strength of the national and patriotic consciousness of all the children of East Timor'. For *maubere* nationalists to turn one's back on the struggle is to renounce membership in the national family. It is to 'betray, and vilify the blood that covers this sacred and beloved Homeland' (Gusmão 2000b:94).

In *maubere* nationalist thought the legacy of resistance carries with it the moral duty to honour the historical *maubere* memory by sacrificing oneself to the struggle for nation. Gusmão (2000b:103) argues that

> this *Maubere* consciousness, the historical identity, proper and genuinely *Maubere*, does not bow before massacres, persecution, banishment or torture. It is for this identity that the struggle is affirmed, with blood and death. The *Maubere* People accepted all the sacrifices demanded of them and will continue to accept what is necessary to preserve that which has been so zealously sought and guarded under the protection of the people's *luliks* (sacred objects) and constantly relived through the oral tradition. This is a sacred patrimony, a sacred heritage that our ancestors were able to bequeath and leave to us: *the*

consciousness that we are a people and that we are making our own history! [italics original].

A common theme in nation-building is to honour by one's own deeds the memory of those who have fought for the nation. Gusmão (2000b:86) states that,

> participation in the struggle for national liberation is a moral duty and, above all, it is a political and historical obligation...This moral and political duty comes not only from current events, but from a history and long tradition of independence struggles.

He suggests that history places a moral imperative upon the youth of East Timor to continue the struggle by invoking the nation's fallen heroes. Gusmão (2000b:89) asserts 'all children of East Timor must keep alive the aspirations of our fearless people!'. Furthermore,

> the youth is the promising force of our people; the youth is the hope of constructing our Homeland; the youth is the guarantee of the future of our nation...our elders, our fathers, are giving you the duty to continue this struggle (Gusmão 2000b:107).

Maubere nationalism holds that not to respond to this duty would be to 'insult the river of blood that continues to flow into the soil of our Homeland' (Gusmão 2000b:89). This sense of duty is like that of the child to its parent or the faithful to God. In *maubere* nationalist thought it is the filial duty of the children of Timor, to subsume their needs to those of the homeland, the pious duty of the faithful nationalist to commit his or her life to the service of the sacred nation.

Sacrifice is a prominent trope in nationalist imaginings (Anderson 1983; Elshtain 1992; 1993; Poole 1985). In the context of nationalist wars, Anderson (1983:16) asks 'what makes the shrunken imaginings of recent history... generate such colossal sacrifices?'. Elshtain (1993:160) suggests that young men go to war to die for their country, to sacrifice their own body for that of the body politic, rather than to kill, to give something one values, one's life, to something one values more, one's nation. Anderson (1983:16) argues that it is the 'deep, horizontal comradeship' of national imagining that inspires millions not so much to kill as to die for their nation. Anderson (1983:229) notes that nations inspire self-sacrificing love that is expressed through the music, literature and art that make up the cultural products of the nation. Elshtain (1993:164) posits that the celebration in national culture of the soldier's sacrifice for his homeland, which is dearer to him than his own life, evinces a similarity to the willingness of the martyrs to die for their faith. Through the act of sacrifice, the homeland, an object of love, becomes a sacred homeland, an object of devotion, the land of martyrs.

Sacrifice, in Western thought, finds its roots in religious acts of supplication to gods or a god.

Sacrifice *n.* ME [O Fr. F .L *sacrificium* rel. to *sacrificus*, f. *sacer* sacred, holy + -*ficus* -FIC]

1 The ritual killing (and frequent burning of the body) of an animal or person, or the offering of a material possession to a god, in propitiation or homage; the practice of doing so.

2 A person or thing offered in sacrifice.

3 *Theol* **a** The Crucifixion as Christ's offering of himself in propitiation for human redemption. **b** The Eucharist regarded as an offering of the bread and wine in union with the body and blood of Christ, or as an act of thanksgiving.

4 the giving of something valued or desired, esp. one's life, for the sake of something regarded as more important or worthy (Brown 1993:2663).

Sacrifice, an offering made to a sovereign entity, a god or gods, is a prominent motif in many religions. Self-sacrifice is performed with a higher purpose than one's own preservation, for the very act of self-sacrifice, of necessity, means one's death. Elshtain (1993:163) argues that religious concepts have permeated political thought, with sacrifice assuming a 'magical force'. This force renders sacrifice obligatory. The power of the sacrificial act lies not in one's choice, but in the perceived lack of choice. Anderson (1983:132) notes that there is little or no glory in dying for 'the Labour Party or the American Medical Association, or even Amnesty International'. One has a choice in these political associations. One does not choose one's country of birth (Bauman 1992:684). It is destiny, the resultant sacrifice the product of fate. In his message to *maubere* youth, Gusmão (2000b:86) makes repeated reference to the moral duty of the Children of Timor to die for the *maubere* nation: 'the vile aggressions and the criminal occupation of our Homeland are, for the *guerilheiros*...the political basis of their motivation and their firm determination to die for their Homeland' [italics original]. Elsewhere he argues that 'to die for [the *maubere* homeland] will constitute a duty for every child of East Timor' (Gusmão 2000b:122). For Gusmão the nation becomes the sovereign entity[6] to which the sacrificial offering is made. One is born onto the soil and of the ancestors of the homeland. Free will is removed, sacrifice is duty, and duty is destiny.

Crucial to an understanding of sacrifice for nation is the relationship between the national homeland and the sacred. Bruce Kapferer (1988:1) suggests that nationalism functions as a religion, elevating the nation to a realm above politics. Gusmão (2000b:126) concludes his message by reminding his audience, 'Your identification as true children of East Timor signals a religious commitment that is at the same time political'. Although he is referring to the identification of the *maubere* nationalist movement with the Catholic Church, he is also arguing that the resistance is a 'manifestation of patriotism and faith' (Gusmão 2000b:126). He suggests that the *maubere* nationalist struggle is an expression of faith, the *maubere* nation the object of devotion. Kapferer (1988:1) refers to nationalist politics as the 'religion of nationalism'. By this he does not mean that nationalism is religious as a result of the nexus with a particular religion, be it *maubere* identification with Catholicism, the link between Japanese nationalism and Shinto, or the role of Buddhism in Sinhalese nationalism. Rather, Kapferer (1988:5) claims that nationalism, including secular nationalism, is religious in its form. The political is shrouded in imagery that lifts it from the mundane to the sacred. For *maubere* nationalists, the Falintil fighter is thus elevated from a mere guerrilla fighter to 'the glorious Falintil' (Gusmão 2000b:85), independence becomes 'the sacred objective' (Gusmão 2000b:90), the nation the 'sacred and beloved Homeland' (Gusmão 2000b:94).

Beloved youth and *maubere* patriots

> Beloved Youth and *Maubere* Patriots…you are the vigorous blood of our people and the promise of the future of our beloved Homeland, East Timor (Gusmão 2000b:86) .

Gusmão asserts that the fate of East Timor rests on the patriotic deeds of the youth of the nation. Children are the hope for the national future. Gusmão (2000b:107) states that children of pre-school age have worked for the resistance:

> They are living examples of courage, living examples of the struggle, living examples of a conscience that is transmitted from parents to children—from the massacred parents to the orphans who survive—this conscience runs in the *Maubere* blood in our veins, impregnates our flesh and penetrates our bones and our innermost being!

For him children symbolise the continuity of the struggle. They are born of the past, live in the present and are bearers of the future. They transmit the familial legacy into the future as they remodel their present into a future unrecognisable to their parents. Dutiful children are the physical manifestation of their parents' yearnings, a vehicle through which the parents are able to vicariously live unfulfilled dreams. Similarly, the children of the nation embody the hope for the national future. Through nationalist ideology that employs familial imagery they are called upon to be dutiful, willing to sacrifice the self, their own blood if necessary, for the collective national good in order to secure the *maubere* homeland and, true to their *maubere* consciousness, uphold the dreams of the parent nation.

An enduring image of the *maubere* struggle is that of a young Timorese boy, arms held aloft, one fist clenched, the other hand forming a victory sign, marching in front of a banner bearing Falintil symbols and calling for national liberation. His face betrays a mixture of fear and defiance as he marches from the Motael Church to the Santa Cruz Cemetery on 12 November 1991. He was killed by Indonesian soldiers that day in what has become known as the Santa Cruz Massacre.[7] Young people have come to represent what could arguably be called the second generation of the East Timorese resistance against the Indonesian occupation (Exposto 1996:33; Gomes 1996). A large number of youth organisations[8] have been directly involved in the resistance. Some of these groups were directly administered by the Executive Committee of Fretilin/CNRM/CNRT[9] for the Clandestine Front.[10] Others were not affiliated with any particular political party. In addition, traditionally conservative organisations such as the Boy Scouts have played critical roles in actions such as demonstrations against the Indonesian occupation. Gomes (1996:115)[11] argues that the youth organisations are guided by the following basic principles:

1. Never desert the sacred ideal of our people, which is the right to self-determination and independence;

2. Make use of the sacred values of the *maubere* ancestors as a source of inspiration in search of a better future for our motherland;

3. Be the strength of our future, the hope of tomorrow and for the times to come in East Timor.

In the language used by Gusmão a decade earlier, Gomes (1996:116) declares:

> The Timorese youth have inherited a unique capacity for patriotism and nationalism in the face of any foreign occupation. Hundreds and thousands of our young people from all political and social categories, have embarked on the great crusade for independence of our motherland.

Many of the young people who were active within the resistance and in actions such as the demonstration at the Santa Cruz cemetery had not been born when Indonesia invaded East Timor in 1975. These are young people who have not known anything other than life under Indonesian rule and who have been educated within the Indonesian education system. The 'hearts and minds' rhetoric of the Indonesian government which sought to normalise the Indonesian presence in the consciousness of East Timorese who have grown up under Indonesian occupation, to impose an Indonesian identity upon them, and to undermine East Timorese nationalist sentiment, has been roundly dismissed by the vast majority of young East Timorese. The coalescence of East Timorese

nationalism since the Indonesian invasion in December 1975 is overwhelmingly
a reaction against the widespread and brutal oppression perpetrated against the
East Timorese by the Indonesian occupation (Arenas 1998:14). There are few
East Timorese who have not directly suffered as a result of the actions of the
Indonesian military occupation of East Timor (Ramos-Horta 1999:14). Arenas
(1998:4) argues that through the Indonesian education system and other social
institutions the East Timorese have been provided with a model against which
to make a claim to a distinctive *maubere* national identity. He suggests that
although the presence of two different cultural groups is not enough to engender
nationalist sentiment,[14] a new 'supra-collective' (Arenas 1998:4) national identity
has evolved that has selected elements of East Timorese culture, in particular
language and religious affiliation, which mark the *maubere* identity as distinctive
in the face of the assimilationist policies of the Indonesian occupation. The
maubere identity has become 'as real as the previous, more traditional one'
(Arenas 1998:4).

For young East Timorese nationalists, the Indonesian language has become
a vehicle for access to tertiary education[13] and modernity, including nationalist
thought, paralleling the experiences of the Indonesian nationalists in their struggle
against Dutch colonialism (Anderson 1993; Arenas 1998; Carey 1997). Despite
the ineligibility of known resistance sympathisers for university scholarships,
many East Timorese studying in Indonesia were active within the resistance,
utilising the access they had to communications technology outside of East Timor
to disseminate information about the situation in East Timor. Furthermore, study
was not simply for personal gain. Gusmão reminded his audience of students:
Your educational development should have the objective of serving your
Homeland! (2000b:106). Quentiliano Mok, a member of the nationalist youth
organisation RETENIL,[14] echoes the sentiments expressed by Gusmão to argue
'[d]efending the rights of the *maubere* people is a sacred duty for all the sons and
daughters of *maubere*. It is to be carried out boldly, selflessly and relentlessly.
Students and young people are an integral part of the *maubere* people' (Mok
1996:106). Many regarded education as a precious resource, a public good, to be
employed in the struggle for the *maubere* nation. All 'Children of Timor' were
expected to contribute to the struggle for the *maubere* national family, utilising all
resources available to them, be they Falintil guerrillas waging a war of resistance
from the mountains or students studying in the diaspora.

Homeland or death

'Homeland or death!'[15] has been Fretilin's guiding slogan since its inception.
Hage (1993:75) suggests that 'being a national(ist) is a question of mere being'.
For the nationalist, being, living and dwelling are intimately connected with

national being. This being is a collective being, a 'we-talk' (Bauman 1992:678). It is, however, a particular form of collectively, grounded in territory and identity. In the context of East Timor to be *maubere* is to hold the promise of national being. *Maubere*, as an identity, is expressed through individuals but only gains its legitimacy, its being, thorough collective expression.[16] The *maubere* nationalist struggle against the Indonesian occupation of East Timor is a struggle for the right to national being. To permanently lose the *maubere* homeland through acquiescence to Indonesia's occupation of East Timor would preclude *maubere* being, where that being is tied to a consciousness of struggle and nation-building. It would mean that the *maubere* cease to be national, indeed, cease to be.

National being is intimately connected with international being. Hage (1993:77) argues that national liberation struggles are less about internal powers than they are about the right to determine foreign policy. In the international community of nation-states 'only those peoples can come under our notice which form a state' (Friedrich Hegel cited in Hage 1993:77). To have a state of one's own confers upon a people the 'illusion of "having control over their destiny" or "self determination"' (Hage 1993:78). In explaining the motivation for the continued struggle, Gusmão (2000b:90) writes:

> Our people resist because they reject integration. Our people resist because they want to live free and independently. Our people resist because they want to be masters of their own destiny. Our heroic people will continue to resist to achieve their sacred objective: national independence.

He continues: 'The people of East Timor only wish to live freely and independently, to simply be their own masters and the owners of our poor but beloved land' (Gusmão 2000b:115). An East Timorese nationalist simply states: 'Life or death: Independence!' (*Scenes from an occupation* 1999). National independence signifies much more than freedom from brutality and oppression. It is the right to political and cultural being, a right many *maubere* nationalists deemed worth dying for. In putting the case against autonomy within Indonesia, Gusmão (2000b:94) states:

> The Falintil guerrillas…prefer to die fighting…I have the utmost confidence that you also, Beloved Youth and *Maubere* Patriots, will not accept the offer of a golden prison in exchange for the fundamental freedoms of the people of East Timor!

The fundamental freedoms of which he speaks are the right to self determination, the right to national and international being.

Hage (1993:74) argues that 'war [is] a process of nation-building within a process of disintegration'. The homeland is the 'sacred objective' (Gusmão 2000b:90) that *maubere* nationalists have been struggling to achieve since the

Indonesian invasion of East Timor in December 1975. War places the nation in the international arena of nation-states. In war, the nation gains recognition (Elshtain 1993:163). War provides a field in which difference is amplified. Nation-building is invigorated by the stark distinctions drawn between people during war. Indeed Gusmão (2000b:102–103) states:

> The war of opposition to Portuguese domination and the particular presence of colonialism were...factors that assured the continuity of our own history and the unique identity of the East Timorese people. This identity carries on, perpetuated by ten years of blood spilt by the Indonesian military occupation.

Hage (1993:99) notes that while the 'other', the enemy, is envisaged as thwarting the nationalist's goal of attaining nationhood, it is the presence of an identifiable threat that renders the imagining of nation possible. Hage's 'other' need not be an external 'other' such as, in the case of *maubere* nationalism, the Portuguese colonial presence or the occupying Indonesian military. There can be an internal 'other' such as UDT supporters during the civil war[17] that followed the UDT coup (see Dunn 1996; Ramos-Horta 1987; Jolliffe 1978) or East Timorese pro-integrationists[18]. As Henderson (1999:17) points out, despite the strength of *maubere* nationalism East Timor had never been completely united.

Nation-states present themselves as a unified active subject within the international field of nation-states, as actors representing the collective will of the individual subjects who comprise the state (Hage 1993:82–83). To do this, they must generate a consensus among the individual national subjects, requiring either the domestication or elimination of the 'other'. Domestication of its internal 'other' (as distinct from Indonesians in East Timor) has been a specific focus of *maubere* nationalism since its inception. Thus the change from ASDT to Fretilin was in part an attempt to distance *maubere* nationalism from a party-based structure, making it more accessible to all East Timorese regardless of political affiliation. It was further in evidence with the short-lived coalition formed between UDT and Fretilin in 1975 and the various restructures of the *maubere* resistance that have occurred since the 1980s. Of particular note is the restructure of the Fretilin-affiliated CNRM (*Counsel Nacional Resistance maubere,* National Council of Maubere Resistance) in 1998 to form a non-partisan umbrella group charged with directing the nationalist resistance. The term *maubere* was dropped from the name, replacing it with 'Timorese' to create the CNRT. The aim was to make the organisation accessible to ever widening circles of East Timorese, particularly the UDT.[19] This process continues to this day with attempts, at the political level at least, to bring about reconciliation between pro-integrationists active in the militias that rampaged through the territory in a spree of murder, rape, looting, mass deportation and destruction after the announcement of the result of the Popular Consultation in September 1999 and those who suffered at their hands. Elimination of the internal 'other', however, may also be deemed a necessary part of nation-building. With the betrayal of Fretilin by the UDT during the UDT coup, domestication gave way to elimination. The mid to late 1970s saw revenge, including imprisonment, torture and summary execution, exacted against those perceived to be traitors to the *maubere* nationalist cause. 'Homeland or death!' can apply not only to those willing to die for the homeland, but those whose actions are perceived to imperial national survival.

The 'sacred and beloved Homeland' (2000b:94) to which Gusmão refers is a homeland with a special character. It is not an imported modern model that provided the motivation which invigorated the protracted struggle against the brutality of the Indonesian military occupation. While the *maubere* nationalists were fighting for a homeland that will take the form of a modern nation-state, they do not envisage it to be a Portuguese mini-state. Gusmão (2000b:103) explains:

> We energetically repudiate that the struggle and the suffering of our people can be limited to 'the preservation of the Portuguese culture' and it is our repudiation that constitutes the principle defining aspect of the *Maubere* People's historical identity.

Kapferer (1988:20) suggests that national being is constituted through cultural artefacts, legend and ritual informed by the logic of myths with resonance in the lives and psychology of the people of the nation. *Maubere* nationalists fought and died not simply for the right to control their own sovereign state (although this is most certainly part of their motivation). They resisted Indonesian domination for the right to culturally constitute a *maubere* homeland, as a place of safety, succour and national being. In an appeal for calm in February 1999 in response to the build up of armed so-called militia Gusmão (1999) states: 'We were forced to fight this war in order to achieve peace which can only be assured by total independence'. As Gusmão (2000b:122) later noted:

> The objective we pursue is simple; the objective for which we fight and give our lives is simple, but sacred: independence for our Homeland and freedom for our people! And for this objective we will pay any price necessary: our independence or our total extermination!.

On this reading the choice is a stark one: homeland or death!

Endnotes

1   Not all East Timorese identify as *maubere*. Some reject the term because of its associations with Fretilin, others because of its associations with colonial oppression (see Niner 2000b:14).

2   One of the ethno-linguistic groups which comprise East Timor's population.

3   A Tetum word which is loosely translated into English as 'war'.

4   Brotherhood is defined as, among other things, 'an association of equals for mutual help' (Brown 1993:289).

5   The ballot conducted under United Nations auspices offering the people of East Timor a choice between independence or autonomy within Republic of Indonesia.

6   It is of note that throughout the text Gusmão capitialises Homeland, akin to the capitalisation of God.

7   See Cox and Carey (1995) and Pinto and Jardine (1997) for a full account.

8   These include, among others, the Association of Timorese Students, formerly the Organisation of Young Catholic Students of East Timor formed under the Fretilin umbrella, the Falintil-operated Clandestine Intervention Front, the East Timor Youth Organisation and the National Resistance of East Timorese Students (Gomes 1996:118–119).

9   CNRM, Concelho Nacional da Restistancia Maubere, National Council of Maubere Resistance, formed in 1987 as the overarching political body combining Fretilin and Falintil. Restructured in 1998 to include UDT, it dropped the term *maubere*, which it replaced with 'Timorese' (see Niner 2000b).

10 A decentralised network of small cells and youth, women's and religious groups working in supprot of the resistance. For a detailed account see Pinto and Jardine (1997).

11 A former member of the Clandestine Front. His cell, made up primarily of young people, was one of the largest (Pinto and Jardine 1997:98).

12 Here he points out that there was little nationalist development under 500 years of Portuguese colonialism (see Arenas 1998; Traube 1995).

13 As a part of the Indonesian education policy thousands of East Timorese students were granted scholarships to study in Indonesian universities. The conditions of the scholarships were stringent, requiring, among other things, that the student not be involved in the anti-Indonesian resistance.

14 *Restencia Nacional dos Estudantes de Timor Leste*, National Resistance of East Timorese Students, formed as a bulwark against the adoption of Indonesian political ideology by East Timorese students studying in Indonesia. It was vociferous within the international community in its defence of East Timorese independence.

15 Homeland is translated from the Portuguese word *patria*, which might more correctly be translated as fatherland. Other variations of this slogan are 'Independence or death!' and 'Motherland or death'.

16 This is not to suggest that *maubere* identity is internally monolithic.

17 See Dunn (1996) and Jolliffe (1978) for a detailed account.

18 Supporters of incorporation of East Timor into Indonesia.

19 See Niner (2000b) for a concise overview.

Homeland and national belonging beyond borders: Filipino domestic workers and transmigrants as a global nation

Claire Kelly

Introduction

Transnational processes have extended national belonging from the geographically bounded community of the Philippines to overseas Filipinos, constituting a global Filipino nation. This chapter focuses on labour migrants, or Overseas Filipino Workers (OFWs),[1] in particular female domestic workers, who are faced with conflicting discourses of identity in the process of nation-building. Transnationalism empowers labour migrants to cope with unsavoury conditions in their countries of residence, but does not liberate them from the discursive practices of their home state. The process of deterritorialised nation-state building (Basch, Schiller & Blanc 1994), relies on the Philippines state extending national discourses to enlist its overseas workers in political and social processes. It has been argued that, in this arrangement, constructions of national identity and belonging depend *more* on the discursive practices of states than on traditional notions of roots, geographical origins and bounded communities (Basch, Schiller & Blanc 1994), challenging the idea that globalisation signals post-nationalism (Kearney 1991). Transmigrants thus are people who take the state with them wherever they go (Basch, Schiller & Blanc 1994). As an example of this, I look at the formation of 'virtual' communities of Filipinos on the internet, to demonstrate that while these, and other, 'grass-roots' communities may offer members a space in which to question the circumstances of their migration, they are not inherently liberating nor free from nationalistic discourses of identity.

Growing international migration sees a significant proportion of the Filipino population geographically dispersed. In December 2003 there were 7,763,178 Filipinos living overseas (POEA 2003). Of these, 3,385,001were on temporary employment contracts. Globally, international migration has been diversified and 'sped up' by the infrastructure and technological innovations accompanying modernity (Giddens 1990). The increasing migration of people from 'Third World' to 'First World' countries, or from 'South' to 'North', is a relatively recent component of globalisation. Increasingly, this type of migration is feminised, as women carry out what Sassen (2003) calls survival circuits, patterns of migration for work made necessary by the increasing debt crises and high unemployment in their home countries. These migratory circuits are feminised because the predominantly available jobs (nannying, nursing, domestic work and prostitution) are considered to be 'female' jobs and because, in situations of poverty, more often than not it is women who are forced to bear the burden of international debt (Enloe 2000).

Labour migration from the Philippines is feminised. In 2002, 69% of newly hired OFWs were women (POEA 2002). Almost half of their jobs were in the service sector. OFWs work in every corner of the globe, with the largest number in middle eastern countries, followed by Asia and Europe (POEA 2003, figure for temporary contract workers). In host countries, migrant domestic worker communities are overwhelmingly female. Of Filipino transmigrant workers in Asia, women outnumber men by 12 to one (WIN 1995). In Italy, 78.3% of Filipino migrants are female (Parreñas 2001b). Immigration regulations in the host countries vary, but the main trend is in temporary migration of single women for contract-based work.

For female Filipino transmigrants, 'survival circuits' are strongly influenced by structural forces, including the international debt crisis, political acts of the sending and receiving states (for example, the marketing of Filipinos as 'great workers', and immigration controls that prevent social integration of working migrants), and the business infrastructure and entrepreneurs who make up the 'maid trade' (Chin 1998). Filipino women migrate to assist the repayment of international debt (Arao 2004; Sassen 2003) (which, in 2001, stood at US $55.3 billion), and to improve the standard of living in a country where 36.8% of the population live below the poverty line (WBG 2003, figure for 1997). The consequent movement of female workers across the globe has challenged traditional concepts of identity and community typically determined by geographical belonging, or 'rootedness' (Malkki 1992). It has forced us to consider new types of communities that may be characterised by their diversity of origin, geographical dispersion, impermanence and shared characteristics of diaspora.

Just as migration has become an inseparable component of Filipino identity, the remittances from Filipino labour migrants are now a mainstay of the Philippines economy. International migration was originally intended only as a temporary measure to resolve an unemployment crisis and generate capital for development through foreign currency exchange (Raj-Hashim 1994). Now, however, the OFW industry supplies the largest single source of foreign capital (Llorito 2003). In 2002, remittances from documented OFWs totaled US$7.189 billion, and in 2003 increased to US$7.639 billion (BSP 2004). Remittances are also directly linked to increased GDP, as remittance money is typically used by families in the Philippines to purchase consumer goods, an area of the economy that has been steadily growing concurrently with international migration (Llorito 2003). Recently re-elected President Gloria Macapagal Arroyo is an enthusiastic proponent of out-migration, and under her administration the OFW industry has grown.

The most recent round of figures from the Philippines Overseas Employment Administration shows that around three quarters of newly hired, unskilled OFWs were service workers (POEA 2002). In the current phase of globalisation, the service industry has exploded, with a trend of flexible, feminised labour (Standing 1998). Sassen (2003) shows that in 'global cities' in 'First World' and newly industrialised countries hosting the technological and business infrastructure that is central to globalisation, immigrant labour in the service industries is crucial to the continuation of that infrastructure. The 'maid trade' is therefore not only an essential component of the Philippines economy but a critical component of economies in 'First World' countries. Interviewed on an Australian current affairs radio program, Philippines Secretary of Labour Patricia Sto Thomas explained the way in which the labour of Filipino women is vital to the global economy:

> If all the Filipino maids in Hong Kong went back tomorrow you might see a lot of things stopping there. If our nurses left for back home in the United States you might see a crisis in the hospital service. If you did the same thing in Saudi Arabia I think you will see a stoppage of critical services in those areas. We are proud that they command the respect of their employers and that they are helping to build a world economy that is founded on competence, loyalty, and yes even love for the people they work for (Thomas 2003).[2]

In 'global cities', the labour force has been supplemented by an expendable group of women not previously engaged in wage labour. This influx of women into what was previously a male-dominated arena is often heralded as a win for feminism. But it is, in actuality, only possible because of the drudgery of low-paid immigrant domestics who maintain the households of these new workers, mind their children and care for their elderly and sick family members (Sassen 2003). For immigrant domestic workers, it is questionable whether their entry into wage labour is a liberating experience.

Away from home, migrant Filipino domestic workers struggle in a world where traditionally, constructions of national identity are tied to geographic belonging (Malkki 1992). By constructing narratives of return and embellishing ideas of 'home', some women build for themselves coping mechanisms that are tied intimately to a sense of unbelonging, the painful experience of family separation, and their concerns for the future (Constable 1999). A number of important ethnographies have focused on the tensions for migrants engendered by this 'non-belonging' in the host country, or 'in-betweenness' (see Constable 1997; 1999; Parreñas 2001a; 2001b; Yeoh & Huang 2000). Parreñas (2001a) refers to such a state as the 'dislocation of non-belonging', because of which a 'sense of constant discomfort' shapes the experience of migrants in their country of residence. She shows that one way of coping is to construct myths of homecoming, in which migrants see themselves returning to the Philippines wealthy and socially mobile. Constable (1999) found that migrants who had managed what she calls the 'dualistic self' (belonging in two places) were less ambivalent about their return home. For other temporary migrant workers in Constable's study, dreams of returning home had remained unfulfilled, as they were often faced with changed family conditions, as well as being forced to undergo the pain of family separation again.

In addition to this sense of unbelonging, migrant Filipino domestic workers also face marginalisation in the host country. In conditions of globalisation, international migration poses a substantial challenge to national identity and citizenship, and as a result, the awarding of citizenship has become increasingly bureacratised and exclusive. Along with refugees and asylum seekers, 'unskilled' (not professional) migrant workers bear the brunt of anti-immigration policies. Host countries typically prefer to accept migrant workers on temporary contracts and visas linked to their work, discouraging reproduction, family reunification and the right to permanent citizenship (Parreñas 2001b).[3] In this process, migrant workers, prohibited from full admission into the national communities in which they work, act as a stop-gap for fluctuating and stratified labour markets. At the same time they perform work that nationals are not obliged to do (Sassen 2003), contribute to the modernisation projects of developing countries, and provide a visible boundary-marker between the new middle classes and the remainder of the population, signifying modernity and development (Chin 1998).

In public and in private, the behaviour of Filipino domestic workers is scrutinised and regulated. Within the household in which they labour, domestic workers are monitored and disciplined by the household head, usually the middle-class wife. As Constable explains:

> Most employers view their domestic workers—and expect those workers to view themselves—as 'maids' at all times, but especially in their employer's homes. A worker must obey her employer's rules, even at night, and in her own room. She may be told when and where to bathe, what time to go to bed, and what she can and cannot wear. Only on her day off is she at all free to express herself outside of the role as domestic worker. But even then, she does so under the watchful eye of the public (Constable 2003:119–20).

Often, disciplinary actions against the maid metamorphose into outright abuse (Anderson 2003; Chin 1998; Hassan 2004).[4] Governments may be considered complicit in this abuse by not adequately protecting the rights of migrant workers. This regulatory failure to protect migrants has been considered a form of structured violence against women (Piper 2003).

In the public sphere, migrants struggle with conflicting discourses of Filipino identities. The Philippines government constructs its OFWs as economic heroes (Constable 1997), ambassadors and investors. Employment agencies market domestic workers as commodities, and encourage employers to regard them so, offering free delivery, free replacements, free servicing and discounted rates.[5] Workers may be ranked according to characteristics such as nationality, regional background, skin colour, religion and other cursory attributes.[6] Employers are encouraged to train and educate workers, who are represented as childlike, culturally inferior and malleable. Finally, host government policies on domestic workers cast them as morally dubious and waywardly sexual, and encourage employers and members of the public to contribute to the task of surveillance.

How do migrant domestic workers cope with their commodification on the global market? How do they rise above marginalisation in the workforce in the host country, and their subordinate status within their employer's household? Identifying with other migrants as a diaspora can play a significant role (Barber 1997, Parreñas 2001b, Yeoh & Huang 2000). Nonini and Ong (1997:18), in their study of Chinese transnationalism, describe the Chinese diaspora as defined by "a pattern that marks a common condition of communities, persons and groups separated by space, an arrangement, moreover, that these persons see themselves as sharing'. As described earlier, narratives of home and return represent this diasporic identity. It should not, however, be assumed that a 'diasporic identity' inherently has reactionary potential.

Grassroots organisations representing diasporic Filipinos may not necessarily offer an alternative Filipino identity to that promoted by the Philippines state. For example, Chang and Groves (2000) researched women's groups connected to the church and to domestic workers' shelters in Hong Kong. They argue that the groups' response to the negative stereotyping of Filipino women and of domestic workers in Hong Kong was to take upon themselves the responsibility of self-monitoring. They constructed a new 'ethic' of service that shaped their identities as morally responsible women who served the Church, their family, their community and their country.[7] Membership of the groups required adherence to strict rules about public behaviour and friendships, rules that were seen as fundamental to maintaining the moral integrity of the group. Chang and Groves thus argue that these groups functioned as an extension of the state. Consequently, as Yeoh and Huang (2000: 415) warn, it is wise to 'tread cautiously on grounds which claim diaspora as an in-between space or subject position that liberates the individual from hegemonic power relations (whether spun by the state, capitalism, or patriarchy)'. In reality, the fact of belonging to the Filipino labour migrant diaspora can endear members to Filipino politics.

The global Filipino nation is characterised by its transnational qualities. Transnationalism can help us theorise questions of community, identity and national belonging in an era of globalisation, 'travelling cultures' (Clifford 1992) and cultural hybridity, where identity and national belonging has become fluid and mobile. In *Nations unbound*, Basch and colleagues suggest that previously bounded communities are now transcending geographical borders, while retaining political and social links to the homeland. For them, transnationalism is:

> the process by which immigrants forge and sustain multi-stranded social relations that link together their societies of origin and settlement. We call these processes transnationalism to emphasise that many immigrants today build social fields that cross geographic, cultural and political borders (Basch, Schiller & Blanc 1994:6).

Filipinos across the globe maintain links with their homeland and with communities in other locations, and thereby comprise a transnational community. For domestic workers in the global Filipino nation, transmigration is the norm, migration is rarely unilinear (Basch, Schiller & Blanc 1994), and return and circular migration are more common than not (Sassen 1998).

Migrant Filipino domestic workers participate in building transnational social fields, maintaining flows of goods, communication and people between the multiple sites in which they reside, facilitated by networks of family and friends. These 'multi-stranded social relations' (Basch, Schiller & Blanc 1994) link together Filipinos working across the globe, and may transgress multiple borders. They have also led to the entrenchment of transnational households, in which family members are located in two or more nation-states (Parreñas 2003).[8] In addition to relying on links with family and friends to pass on information and material goods, thanks to modern communications technology, Filipino transmigrants living overseas can not only talk on the phone, they can 'chat' in rooms on the internet, contribute to online discussion forums, read news about the Philippines online, send items home via internet gift sites, and remit money to the Philippines electronically. This immediate, electronic transfer of goods and money is now a crucial part of the OFW industry. Transnational connections can also enable Filipinos to circumvent formal channels for securing employment, sending home remittances and gifts, and engaging in alternative income-building practices. Relying on networks of family and friends to obtain employment through 'word of mouth', or personal recommendations, can enable migrant workers to escape the extortionate practices of employment agencies (Anderson 2001). Transnationalism has also been documented in a domestic worker community to provide entrepreneurial individuals with income-generating activities alternative to their domestic work (Parreñas 2001a).

Nevertheless, being away from home and belonging to a transnational community do not necessarily liberate migrant domestic workers from the potentially oppressive discourses of familialism and 'duty' propagated by the home state. This idea can be further elucidated by comparison to another study of transnationalism. In their discussion of Chinese overseas, Nonini and Ong (1997) found that diasporic Chinese, rather than being unfettered by hegemonic power relations, are subjected to what they term 'regimes of truth and power'. For Chinese overseas, these regimes are the Chinese family, the capitalist workplace and the nation-state. In a later article, Nonini (2002) refers to such hegemonic practices as 'territorially based regimes of power and knowledge', arguing that such regimes do indeed transcend the nation-state. I suggest that the same regimes of power and knowledge, originating in the Philippines, extend to Filipino transmigrants. Like Chinese overseas, Filipino transmigrants are subjected to discipline by the nation-state, the capitalist workplace (for domestic workers, the household) and the diasporic community itself.

Though this discipline is intended to minimise the impact of migrant workers on the larger community while maximising their productivity, it can lead transmigrants to adopt a nationally prescribed identity that helps them survive this marginalisation. For this reason, Basch and colleagues suggest that racial barriers in the host country can act as incentives to embrace a transnational identity. Their fieldwork showed that Filipino immigrants in the United States were constantly made aware of their outsider status, regardless of the conditions of their residency or the length of time they had lived there. They argue that for these immigrants, 'the more they come to know America, the more they take up as their own agenda the building of deterritorialised national identities' (Basch, Schiller & Blanc 1994:234). In this respect I would argue that, rather than Filipino transmigrants constructing a new identity defining a community that transcends that of the Philippines (Parreñas 2001b), they are instead taking part in the nation-building practices of the Philippines state, and asserting their belonging to what has become a global nation of Filipinos.

The idea of a global Filipino nation is assisted by the invention of homelands and construction of spaces in which to contest and strengthen ideas of national identity (Appadurai 2002). National identity defines and binds the global Filipino nation. In this respect the nation is as much 'imagined' as it is real. As theorised by Benedict Anderson (1983), an 'imagined political community' is linked by common characteristics of nationality and nationness, which are cultural artefacts produced in a specific historical context. Often conceptualised as a condition of modernity, imagined communities link those present with those absent, in ways made possible by globalisation (Giddens 1990). Transmigrant Filipinos are united in an imagined community by their sense of diaspora, difficult conditions in the host countries and economic duty to the Philippines. For OFWs, the internet and internationally available magazines and newspapers are essential to imagining a global nation of Filipinos. Technological innovations make this possible. As Appadurai (1991) argues, transnational mediascapes can unite dispersed communities, and for Filipino transmigrants, print media and the internet can help to bring together the imagined global community, at the same time representing an idealised version of Filipino national identity. Though overseas workers themselves often create and contribute to these forums, transnational mediascapes are not necessarily liberating for migrant Filipino domestic workers.

Domestic worker magazines can, Parreñas (2001b) argues, 'provide a tangible link connecting migrant Filipino domestic workers in the formation of an imagined global community'. Literature focusing on Filipino domestic workers has deconstructed the role played by international domestic worker magazines.[9] While these publications may allow domestic workers to challenge prejudicial views of themselves aired in the mainstream press, they also function to reinforce ideas of Filipino nationalism, ethics of familialism and economic duty (Chang & Groves 2000; Yeoh & Huang 2000). As such, they may be as regulating as the Philippines government, the employment agency and the employer (Constable 1997). In addition, while offering a forum for workers to voice narratives of displacement and pain at marginalisation in the host country, these magazines offer no critical insight into the politics of their situation (Parreñas 2001b). The same is true for 'virtual' communities on the internet.

A number of online or virtual communities on the internet serve the global nation of Filipinos.[10] These websites offer news from home, categories such as travel, entertainment and health, and migrant-specific services including remittance centres, online gift shopping, email, chat rooms and discussion forums. Forums allow Filipinos worldwide to discuss and debate shared concerns, as well as fostering identification with the global community.[11] Many include a section devoted to OFWs, where workers can have a dialogue about the identity tension engendered by working away from home, the ways in which they cope with family separation, and share stories about the type of work they do and the extent to which they feel accepted in their country of residence. In this way, virtual communities facilitate the maintenance of transnational social fields. They also encourage emotional ties between overseas Filipinos and their homelands, and ask them to identify with the community as a 'virtual home away from home' (Global Nation 2005b). By using these sites, Filipino transmigrants working abroad to send home remittances can resist becoming socially or politically disenfranchised from the homeland.

But while virtual communities hosted on the internet may facilitate the maintenance of transnational social fields, and allow a space to discuss shared characteristics of diaspora, they contain little potential for challenging hegemonic constructions of national identity. Ignacio (2000) carried out unique fieldwork in a virtual community (a newsgroup) of Filipino-Americans on the internet, expecting to find identity constructions free from the dichotomised frameworks characterising grounded notions of female Filipino identity. Instead, she found that Filipino women were sexualised and commodified, as well as being marginalised by the overwhelmingly male majority of newsgroup participants. She concludes that 'real life' prejudices and stereotypes are present in the newsgroup, proving that 'cyberspace' is not as decentring and liberated from grand narratives as has been claimed.

Likewise, internet sites catering for Filipino transmigrants celebrate and promote particular aspects of national identity that have become synonymous with Filipino-ness. Often labour migrants collude in this. For example, Global Nation (2005b) emphasises the 'Great Filipino Worker'. It hosts the 'OFW Spotlight', which regularly features the profile of an OFW, submitted by the subjects. Contributors generally encourage other labour migrants to continue their allegiance to the Philippines, and continue their participation in its nation-building. No doubt this section is intended not only to reward those Filipinos who have been labouring abroad, but also to encourage others to migrate. Another online community especially for labour migrants casts its members as global ambassadors (OFWO 2005b). As well as contributing economically by sending home remittances, labour migrants are encouraged to act as tourist industry representatives by encouraging foreign friends and colleagues to visit the Philippines. The duty of OFWs to their homeland is apparently limitless. The site argues: 'As an OFW, they have been doing a lot of help to the Philippines [sic], but they know they can still do more, Philippines needs them now more than ever!'

It could be argued that the formation of communities for Filipino transmigrants on the internet via portals, discussion lists, newsgroups and forums is a form of grassroots resistance to the dominant political discourse in the home country. However, as with international domestic worker magazines, global communities on the internet tend rather to reinforce these discourses, failing to offer an alternative identity to that of the 'Great Worker' and 'economic hero'. Consequently, I concur with Guarnizo and Smith (1998:24) that the identities offered by transnational communications 'are often no less essentialised than the hegemonic projects of nation-states. Identities forged "from below" are not inherently subversive or counter-hegemonic'. As Ignacio (2000:554) concluded from her study of Filipino internet newsgroups, despite being 'located in a transnational virtual space, they are still based on traditional, boundaried spaces (usually nations)'. Transnationalism, then, does not necessarily liberate migrant Filipino domestic workers from the discursive practices of the home state.[12]

The Philippines project of nation-building relies on enlisting the loyalty of its overseas workers. Nonini and Ong (1997) argue that the Chinese state employs knowledge-power systems to create 'imagined communities' that encompass Chinese living outside the state. The same nation-building rhetoric and processes are used to define the deterritorialised community of Filipinos. Nonini and Ong (1997) point out the importance of deconstructing the discursive tropes used to make concrete the 'regimes of truth' that the home state employs to control the transnational community. This theory can also be applied to the Philippines state's representation of its overseas workers, with consideration of the profitability for the state of extending national belonging beyond national borders. OFWs are crucial to the Philippines for economic and political reasons, and as such the state uses tropes that emphasise national allegiance and national identity, while creating an insoluble link between Filipino-ness and migration.

Government rhetoric conflates being Filipino with being a migrant, and a 'great worker'. The official homepage of the Republic of the Philippines welcomes visitors to the 'home of the Great Filipino Worker' (RP 2005b). Every June, the government sponsors an international Migrant Worker's Day to celebrate the contribution of their OFWs.[13] In 2003, many events held worldwide were deliberately planned to coincide with Philippines Independence Day, making a direct link between national identity and overseas work. The government also hosts the annual Bagong Bayani Awards, rewarding OFWs as the country's 'modern-day heroes' (POEA 2004). The awards are 'a tribute to the significant efforts of OFWs in fostering goodwill among peoples of the world, in enhancing the image of the Filipino as a competent worker, and in contributing to the nation's foreign exchange earnings' (PDLE 2004). To be eligible, entrants must have been OFWs for at least two years. These awards celebrate the migration of Philippine nationals, and reward their overseas labour, while reminding them of their obligation to the homeland.

By celebrating and reinforcing the Filipino-ness of transmigrants, the Philippines state harnesses them to the cause of economic development. In a 2003 speech to overseas Filipinos, President Arroyo referred to the 'strong homing instinct of every Filipino after a long sojourn in a foreign land' to engender economic support for the Philippines:

> ...we know that the majority of the Filipinos who migrated abroad did so for better opportunities, but they continue their allegiance to the Philippines. This continued allegiance is demonstrated by their maintaining contacts and interests in their homeland, and by their intention to retire, own properties and invest their hard-earned money in the country. Our overseas workers have become a powerful force, not only in the economies in which they work and live, but in our economy. In fact, it is to them once again that we call on. We call on the families of our overseas workers to exchange their dollars in the banks so that we can all help to strengthen the peso (Arroyo 2003a).

This demonstrates the discourses of 'allegiance' and 'national belonging' employed by the government to engender the economic support of OFWs. OFWs are constructed as loyal patriots, charged with the responsibility of reinvigorating a homeland suffering from acute poverty and underdevelopment. This may be even more true for female domestic workers, many of whom, through their migration, are fulfilling family obligations as 'dutiful daughters' (Eviota 1992).

In the rhetoric of the Philippine government, OFWs often become more than workers; they become investors. In a speech made to the Filipino-American community in Los Angeles, President Arroyo told her audience:

> Filipino-Americans constitute one-third of overseas Filipinos, but you contribute 71 percent of foreign exchange remittances. This contribution translates to education because we build many schools; it translates as housing because you buy houses for your relatives; it translates to anti-poverty programs in the Philippines because you capitalise [sic] your relatives and you also make philanthropic contributions. That's why I always say that you're not overseas Filipino workers rather you're overseas Filipino investors. I'd like to take this opportunity to renew my call for our overseas Filipino investors to continue to support our economy so that our aspiration of liberating our people from poverty can be fully realized (Arroyo 2003b)

In addition to economic reasons for celebrating a global and transnational Filipino nation, the Philippine state has a political agenda. In *Nations unbound* (1994), Basch, Schiller and Blanc describe the ways in which the Haitian political leader Aristide engendered the support of Haitians living in Canada and the US, referring to them as the '10th department' of Haiti. In the same way, President Arroyo has reached out to overseas Filipinos. In the 2004 national elections, for the first time, Filipinos living outside the Philippines were able to vote, thanks to the enactment of Arroyo's twin electoral reform projects: dual citizenship and absentee voting. These policies were pushed through in 2003 with recognition that over seven million Filipinos living outside the nation constitute a powerful voting bloc. The changes were also lobbied for by groups representing OFWs.[14] Nevertheless, eligibility to vote was conditional. Overseas Filipinos could only register if they declared their intention to return to the Philippines for permanent residence within three years of registration approval (CPCA 2004). As transmigration is the norm for OFWs, this is a difficult compromise.

The overseas voting process extends political belonging beyond the physical boundaries of the Philippines. For Arroyo, taking foreign citizenship does not mean the relinquishing of loyalty to the homeland. A large percentage of overseas Filipinos have taken up permanent residency in the US. As did Aristide for migrant Haitians, Arroyo repeatedly calls on the support of these Filipino-Americans, appealing to their sense of loyalty and duty to the homeland, because 'we know that you continue to love the Philippines even if you're already American citizens' (Arroyo 2003c). The passage of the Dual Citizenship Act and the Absentee Voting legislation ensures the continued political support of Filipino transmigrants, supporting Basch and colleagues' view that, 'in the new world of transnational practices, geographic boundaries are no longer understood to contain all the state's citizens or political processes essential to its perpetuation' (Basch, Schiller & Blanc 1994:269).

Conclusion

The growth of the OFW industry and the strength of government discourse about its OFWs has meant that transmigration for work has become an inseparable part of being Filipino. In addition, the Philippines has come to rely on its networks of labour migrants and permanent residents living across the globe for the perpetuation of Philippines nationalism. The global Filipino nation has become entrenched in the global economy, as well as in the imaginations of Filipino transmigrants. While identifying with others as diasporic may provide migrant Filipino domestic workers with a space in which to share narratives of homeland and identity, this subject position does not liberate its members from the nationalist discourses of the Philippines as a deterritorialised nation-state.

Endnotes

1   Overseas workers from the Philippines are interchangeably referred to as OCWs (Overseas Contract Workers), OFWs (Overseas Filipino Workers) and ODWs (Overseas Domestic Workers). The government's term, OFW, refers only to those 'deployed' workers who have registered with the POEA and have legal documents. As such I have chosen to refer to Filipinos overseas as transmigrants. I intend this to include the three administrative categories of overseas Filipinos: permanent residents, contract workers and undocumented workers or visa overstayers (POEA 2003). When referring only to migrant workers, I have used the term Filipino labour migrants, unless referring to official statistics from the Philippines Overseas Employment Administration (POEA).

2   That Thomas refers to 'love' in this context is not surprising. Domestic workers are often considered different to other migrant labourers in that they are typically attached to a family (and often their employment visa is tied to this arrangement), and are often said to be 'one of the family'. This notion is, however, quickly discarded when delegating undesirable tasks, or when the worker has immigration trouble or is becoming difficult to discipline and as such is more a discourse which aids control (Enloe 2000). In the meantime, this discourse of being part of the family can help to disguise the exploitative nature of the employment relationship, whilst maintaining the idea that the domestic worker performs her work out of love and loyalty to the family. It is useful for the Philippines government to emphasise this 'caring' attribute of Filipinos, because it puts them ahead of other nationalities in the domestic work market.

3   Immigration policies towards contract workers vary from country to country, and cannot be described individually here. For a more detailed comparison of the destination countries for Filipino domestic workers, see Parreñas (2001b). For a close look at the ways in which one state's policies on immigration and reproductive rights impact directly on migrant women, see Cheng's work on Taiwan (2003)

4   For undocumented workers, without the legal protection offered by the host country and their home country, patterns of abuse may be worse. See Zarembka's (2003) article on maids in the USA, and 'modern-day slavery'.

5   These offers can be seen in the advertisements of employment agencies in the classifieds of local newspapers, as well as on their internet sites. For example, see the 'Full Deluxe Package' available from AUK Management in Singapore (AUK nd)

6   See for an example the website of Hong Kong agency Proxy-Maid. It features a chart helping employers to choose the nationality that best suits them (Proxy-Maid nd). Filipinos are 'more hygienic, more organised, and have better communication skills', and are good for taking care of babies. Indonesian maids are notable for 'more loyalty due to their cultural background and characteristics; more obedience because they come from more remote and poorer provinces'. Thai maids are characterised as having poorer language skills but being good at cooking, and always obedient. This style of marketing is common among employment agencies specialising in domestic workers.

7   There were some women in Chang and Groves' study who were able to challenge the dominant paradigm of respectability linked to sexual behaviour and piety— usually part-time workers, and 'tomboys' (lesbians), but these were in a marked minority.

8   Transnational households have become so common among OFWs as to fuel a public debate about the 'care crisis' in the Philippines (Parreñas 2003), and its social and psychological effects on the family members who remain (Cohen 2000).

9   Yeoh and Huang (2000) discuss *Tulay Ng Tagumpay* (or TNT), a church-based monthly magazine available in Singapore and Hong Kong. *Tinig Filipino*, now defunct, was a very popular private magazine edited by a Filipino ex-domestic worker, available internationally (Chang & Groves 2000; Constable 1997; Parreñas 2001b).

10   For example: Global Nation (2005b), GlobalPinoy.com (2005b) and Philstar.com (2005).

11   Some examples of discussion forums (current at the time of writing) are 'Global Filipinos' at Global Pinoy (2005a), Forum at Global Nation (2005a), a forum on the Philippines government portal (RP 2005a), message boards and forums at efilipinos (2005) and a forum at OFW Online (OFWO 2005a)

12   This is not to suggest that there are no dissenting voices to the OFW industry. In fact, local and transnational civil society movements and NGOs play an essential role in advocating for the human rights of OFWs. Rather, I am suggesting that these organisations are not inherently subversive, that Filipino nationalist discourse is itself transnational, and that it is often migrants as well as government agents who take up this discourse.

13   This day, and its nationalist rhetoric, is by no means universally embraced. For example, Migrante International (MI), a Philippines-based organisation that assists OFWs, counters this day with a week-long migrant's protest (MI 2005). MI is directly critical of the Arroyo administration and calls for the President's resignation, arguing that her continued promotion of international migration, but neglect of OFWs, constitutes violence against Filipinos.

14   EMPOWER (2003) brought together the various groups lobbying for overseas voting rights in a single campaign. Their campaign statement is a strongly worded representation of members' passionate attachment to Filipino politics, despite their migration. It demonstrates that deterritorialisation can endear or disenfranchise transmigrants from Filipino politics; as Appadurai (2002:54) argues, deterritorialisation can sometimes create 'exaggerated and intensified senses of criticism or attachment to politics in the home state'.

Migration in Indonesia: recent trends and implications

Graeme Hugo

Introduction

In the massive economic, social and political change experienced in Indonesia over the last decade, population mobility has been a significant cause and consequence. While there is significant regional, ethnic, socio-economic and demographic segmentation in the level and types of population movement, there can be no doubt that across the nation Indonesians are more mobile and range over a wider area in search of job opportunities and now consider opportunities at national and international levels much more than ever before. This chapter seeks to provide a demographic picture of recent changes in population mobility in Indonesia and to discuss some of the major issues associated with those changes. While there are important connections between them, internal and international migration are treated separately.

At the outset it needs to be acknowledged that any review of population mobility in Indonesia is constrained by the limitations of both the available data and the volume of research relating to the causes and consequences of internal and international migration. Firstly, with respect to internal migration,[1] the major source of data is the decennial census of population and housing, which, while useful, has some limitations, in particular:

- The data are only for migration between provinces and the bulk of movement is within provinces.

- It excludes non-permanent migration.

The government has collected information on the participants in the Transmigration Program (Hardjono 1977; 1986) as well as to some extent on internally displaced persons (Hugo 2002a). With respect to international migration, there is little or no information available on flows across borders; nor is there data on stocks of migrants collected at the population census (Hugo 2006a). The Labour Department maintains some statistics on international labour migrants who leave Indonesia through official means, but excludes the significant flow of undocumented migrants. Despite these data limitations it is possible to paint a reasonably indicative picture of contemporary mobility in Indonesia.

Internal movements

Levels of mobility

Any observer of Indonesia over recent decades could not help but have noticed a parametric increase in individual mobility that has occurred, although it is not easy to demonstrate this with the available data. Nevertheless, Table 1 shows that at each census the proportion of Indonesians who had lived in a different province has increased. While females are slightly less likely to have been inter-provincial migrants than males, the gap has narrowed since 1971, reflecting the increasing significance of the migration of women in Indonesia (Hugo 1992). However, census data such as that presented in Table 1 is only the tip of the iceberg of all mobility, which is predominantly intra-provincial and non- permanent and, hence, undetected by the census internal migration questions.

Table 1: Indonesia: measures of migration, 1971–2000

Year	Migration Measure	Males	Females
1971	Percent ever lived in another province	6.29	5.06
1990	Percent ever lived in another province	10.62	9.03
1990	Percent five-year migrants: interprovincial	3.54	3.12
2000	Percent ever lived in another province	10.56	9.57
2000	Percent five-year migrants: interprovincial	3.16	2.96

Source: Indonesian censuses of 1971, 1990 and 2000.

Table 2: Indonesia: number of persons per motor vehicle, 1950–2000

Year	Persons/motor vehicle (including motorcycles)	Persons/motor vehicle (excluding motorcycles)
1950	1,507	1,691
1961	263	447
1971	129	300
1980	38	123
1990	20	64
2000	11	39

Source: Biro Pusat Statistik publications on motor vehicles and length of roads.

Some indication of the increase in personal mobility can be appreciated from Table 2, which shows the massive decline that has occurred in the ratio of people to motor vehicles in Indonesia. While the overlap of private cars has increased, a high proportion of the national fleet is buses and public transport of one kind or another. There has been a proliferation of public transport of varying type, size and, importantly, price that opens up the ability to travel long distances to almost all Indonesians.

Spatial patterns of internal migration

The dominant theme in Indonesian internal migration throughout the 20th century was *Transmigrasi*, the government program to resettle people from densely settled Java and Bali (842 persons per km in 2000) to the less densely settled outer Indonesian islands, mainly Sumatra, Kalimantan, Sulawesi and Papua. Official resettlement programs existed for most of the country and the program was officially closed only in 2000. Table 3 shows the numbers of families moved and Figure 1 their destinations.

Table 3: Number of transmigrants, 1905–98

	Period	Number of families
1905–68		242,774
Repelita I	1969–74	39,436
Repelita II	1974–79	55,083
Repelita III	1979–84	365,977
Repelita IV	1984–89	228,422
Repelita V	1989–94	247,000
Repelita VI	(up to 31 March 1998)	315,495
Total		1,494,187

Source: Mubyarto 2000:6.

Over the period 1900–2000 the proportion of Indonesia's population living in Java fell from 72 to 59%. On the face of it this would appear to be a resounding affirmation of the Transmigration Policy but it is predominantly due to:

• higher levels of fertility in the Outer Islands.

• spontaneous migration from Java to the Outer Islands which is substantially greater than that under official auspices.

Table 4: Migration into and out of Java, 1971, 1980, 1990 and 2000

Java	1971	1980	1990	2000	Percentage change		
					1971–80	1980–90	1990–2000
Total outmigrants	2,062,206	3,572,560	5,149,470	5,380,889	+73	+44.1	+4.5
Total immigrants	1,067,777	1,225,560	2,434,719	2,231,745	+15	+98.7	-8.3
Net migration	-994,429	-2,347,000	-2,714,751	-3,149,144	+136	+15.7	+16.0

Source:　1971, 1980, 1990 and 2000 censuses of Indonesia
Note: Based upon 'most recent' migration data using census question on province of previous residence.

Table 5: Population change in the Jakarta metropolitan area according to different definitions, 1971–2000

Definition	Population				Percentage growth		
	1971	1980	1990	2000	1971–80	1980–90	1990–2000
Special Capital City (DKI) district of Jakarta	4,546,492	6,071,748	8,227,766	8,347,100	33.5	35.5	1.5
DKI Jakarta and urban Bogor, Bekasi and Tanggerang kabupaten	4,838,221	7,373,563	13,096,693	18,085,300	52.4	77.6	45.7
DKI Jakarta, Kotamadya Bogor and kabupaten Bogor, Bekasi and Tanggerang (Jabotabek)	8,374,243	11,485,019	17,105,357	20,438,800	37.1	48.9	19.5

Source: 1971, 1980, 1990 and 2000 Censuses of Indonesia

Figure 1: Destination of transmigrants, 1968–2000

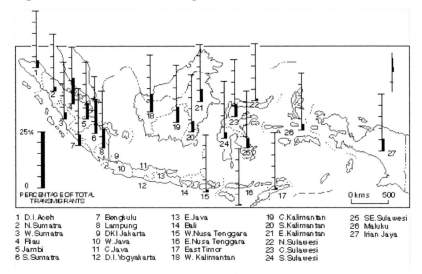

1 D.I.Aceh	7 Bengkulu	13 E.Java	19 C.Kalimantan	25 SE.Sulawesi
2 N.Sumatra	8 Lampung	14 Bali	20 S.Kalimantan	26 Maluku
3 W.Sumatra	9 DKI Jakarta	15 W.Nusa Tenggara	21 E.Kalimantan	27 Irian Jaya
4 Riau	10 W.Java	16 E.Nusa Tenggara	22 N.Sulawesi	
5 Jambi	11 C.Java	17 East Timor	23 C.Sulawesi	
6 S.Sumatra	12 D.I.Yogyakarta	18 W. Kalimantan	24 S.Sulawesi	

Source: RI 1993; 1998; Pramono 2000.

Table 4 shows the migration between Java and the rest of Indonesia over the last three decades. This indicates that:

• outmigration from Java increased rapidly between 1971–1980 and 1990, but more slowly in the subsequent decade;

• inmigration to Java increased slowly in the 1970s but increased in the 1980s and slowed down in the 1990s;

• net migration to the Outer Islands increased rapidly in the 1970s but more slowly in the 1980s and 1990s.

Clearly Java has increased its significance not just as an origin of outmigrants to the Outer Islands but also as a destination for inmigrants from the Outer Islands.

The pattern of inter-provincial migration shown by the 2000 census is depicted in Figure 2. A number of patterns are striking. The first is the high degree of reciprocation of the flows, indicating that there is an important return migration in Indonesia (Hugo 1975). Significantly, Jakarta and West Java are the main destinations of inter-provincial migrants in Indonesia, accounting for 33.6% of all such inmigrants. This reflects the movement to metropolitan Jakarta that has long overspilled its boundaries into the province of West Java.

Table 5 shows the population for three definitions of metropolitan Jakarta—the province boundaries, the extent of continuous built up area and the Jabotabek (Jakarta plus the surrounding Kabupaten of Bogor, Tanggerang and Bekasi and Kotamadya Bogor). There is now more of the Jakarta (as a functioning city) population living outside the boundaries of DKI Jakarta than within it. Indeed Jakarta, with a population of over 20 million, is one of the world's great mega cities (Jones 2004).

Figure 2: Indonesia: major inter-provincial migration according to province of birth from the 2000 census

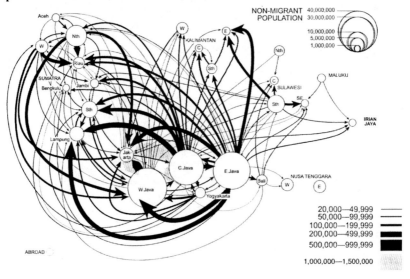

Source: Indonesian census 2000

Urbanisation through redistribution of people from rural to urban areas is a major element in Indonesian internal migration and a process of major economic and social significance in the country. Table 6 shows that the proportion of Indonesians living in areas designated urban[2] increased from 14.8% in 1961 to 42.4% in 2000. In that time, however, the numbers in urban areas increased six times to reach 85,380,627 in 2000. The significance of rural to urban migration is apparent if inter-kabupaten migration data are examined. Figure 3 shows net migration for West Java kabupaten and it can be seen that only the urbanising kabupaten along the Jakarta–Bandung corridor experienced net gains, while the more rural kabupaten experienced net migration loss.

Table 6: Indonesia: urban growth and trends in urbanisation, 1961–2000

Characteristic	Census Year					Percentage Growth per Annum[a]			
	1961	1971	1980	1990	2000	1961-71	1971-80	1980-90	1990-2000
Urban population	14,358,372	20,465,377	32,846,000	55,433,790	85,380,627	+3.61	+5.40	+5.37	+4.41
Rural population	82,660,457	98,874,687	114,089,000	123,813,993	115,861,372	+1.79	+1.63	+0.82	-0.66
Urban (percentage)	14.8	17.2	22.4	30.9	42.4	+1.51	+2.98	+3.27	+3.21
Rural (percentage)	85.2	82.8	77.6	69.1	57.6	-0.29	-0.72	-1.15	-1.80
Total population	97,018,829	119,140,064	146,935,000	179,247,783	201,241,999	+2.08	+2.36	+2.01	+1.16
Urban/rural ratio	0.174	0.207	0.287	0.448	0.737	+1.75	+3.70	+4.55	+5.10

Note: The definitions of urban used in this table are those used in each census referred to. In the 1980 and 1990 censuses this is based on a combined measure including population density, proportion of the population working in non-agricultural occupations, and presence of designated urban facilities (Hugo 1981, 1993a).

a - All percentage growth rates per annum are compound interest rates.

Source: Hugo et al. 1987:89; 1990 and 2000 censuses of Indonesia.

Figure 3: Inter-provincial migration in West Java, 1995

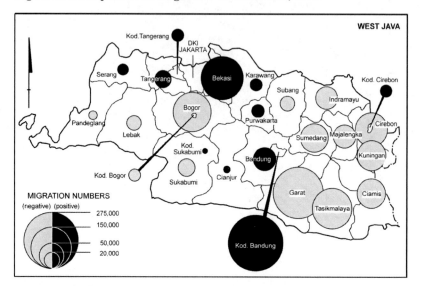

Source: Wahyuni 2000

A few points can be made abut the characteristics of internal migration in Indonesia:

- People of workforce age, especially those in the young adult age groups, are strongly represented in migration figures. This has meant that the youth population is more concentrated in urban areas than the remainder of the population. Hence in 1995, 40.4% of Indonesians aged 20–34 lived in urban areas, compared with 35.9% of the rest of the population.

- Better educated groups are strongly represented in migration figures.

- Women outnumbered men migrating to cities over short distances, but males outnumbered females moving to cities over long distances.

- An increasing stream of movers in recent years has been that of people moving to cities, especially in West Java and Jakarta, to work in factories. This is particularly true of women (Sunaryanto 1998).

- There is more labour market segmentation among female migrants than is the case for males. They are especially concentrated in factory work, domestic work and in the sex/entertainment sector (Hull, Sulistyaningsih and Jones 1998).

- More or less permanent rural to urban area migration is typical of people obtaining work in the formal sector in cities, whereas circular migrants engage in non-permanent circular migration (see next section).

Circulation

However, statistics on internal migration fail to detect most non-permanent movements within Indonesia and it is clear that such mobility has long been of significance in Indonesia (Hugo 1978) and that it has massively increased in scale, complexity and importance in recent years (Collier et al 1993). It predominantly involves people leaving rural areas temporarily and leaving their families behind. Their main destinations are cities, mines, plantations, forestry sites, construction sites and industrial zones like Batam. Some of the key features of contemporary circulation in Indonesia are as follows:

- This type of mobility strategy is highly compatible with work participation in the urban informal sector, as the flexible time commitments allow people the time to circulate to their home village. Similarly, the ease of entry to the urban informal sector is a factor.

- Participation in work in both the urban and rural sectors spreads the risk by diversifying families' portfolio of income earning opportunities.

- The cost of living in urban areas (especially Jakarta) is considerably higher than in rural areas, so that keeping the family in the village and 'earning in the city while spending in the village' allows earnings to go much further.

- Java's transport system is cheap, diverse and allows workers to get to their home village quickly.

- Job options in the village, especially during seasonal increases in demand for labour (such as harvesting time) are able to be kept open. Hence risk can be spread over several sources of income.

- Many informal and formal sector employers in large cities, especially Jakarta, provide barracks type accommodation for workers.

- Often the movement is part of a family labour allocation strategy in which some members are sent out of the village to contribute to the village-based family's income.

- In many cases there is a social preference for living and bringing up children in the village, where there are perceived to be fewer negative, non-traditional influences.

- Social networks are crucial in the development of this form of migration. Most temporary migrants make their initial movement with other experienced migrants or join family or friends established at the destination.

- As is the case with international migration, recruiters and middlemen of various types have played a significant role in the increasing rural to urban migration in Indonesia.

As Collier et al (1993:41) point out:

Often a factory manager will meet with the head of the village to recruit young people for his factory. They sometimes would send a bus in the morning to pick up the workers.

Such a pattern of strong *mandor* (foremen), *calo* (recruiter) and taikong (*agents*) has a long history in Java and has become even more significant in recent years in encouraging migration to both formal and informal sector jobs based in urban areas. Firman (1991), for example, has demonstrated the critical role played by *mandor* in the construction industry in urban Indonesia.

The fact that in most parts of Indonesia circulation is of greater significance than permanent redistribution is evident in Table 7, which is drawn from a study of a Central Java village that investigated both permanent and temporary movement.

Table 7: Population and household heads by residence status in RW°06 Pasawahan village, 1996

Type of residence			Household head				Population	
		Male		Female		Total		Total
Local	145	(26.3%)	11	(6.3%)	156	(21.5%)	639	(30.1%)
Permanent	181	(32.8%)	28	(16.1%)	209	(28.8%)	615	(29.0%)
Temporary	226	(40.9%)	135	(77.6%)	361	(49.7%)	867	(40.9%)
Total	552	(100.0%)	174	(100.0%)	726	(100.0%)	2,121	(100.0%)

Source: Wahyuni 2000

Internally displaced persons

Conflict has been an important cause of population movement in Indonesia both during the early years of Independence (Hugo 1987) and in the late 1990s (Hugo 2002a). More recently the tsunami of December 2004 created 500,000 internally displaced persons. The troubles of the late 1990s, however, created well over a million displaced persons and Figure 4 shows where they were located around 2000. Almost half of these displaced persons were in camps and the rest living with relatives or in other private accommodation. Much of the displacement was from areas that in early Independence years were areas of inmigration of different ethno-religious groups, either through spontaneous migration or through the Transmigration Program. While these conflicts have been put down to religious or cultural clashes, in fact they are much more complex and associated with stark differences in empowerment, access to services and wealth. From a migration perspective it is interesting that many of the IDPs returned to the areas their parents, grandparents or even earlier ancestors left generations ago. Hugo (2006b) has argued that the significance of forced migration in Indonesia has been neglected and shows that this movement has been crucial to urbanisation in Indonesia and in establishing networks along which later spontaneous migrants flowed.

Figure 4: Distribution of internally displaced persons, 2000

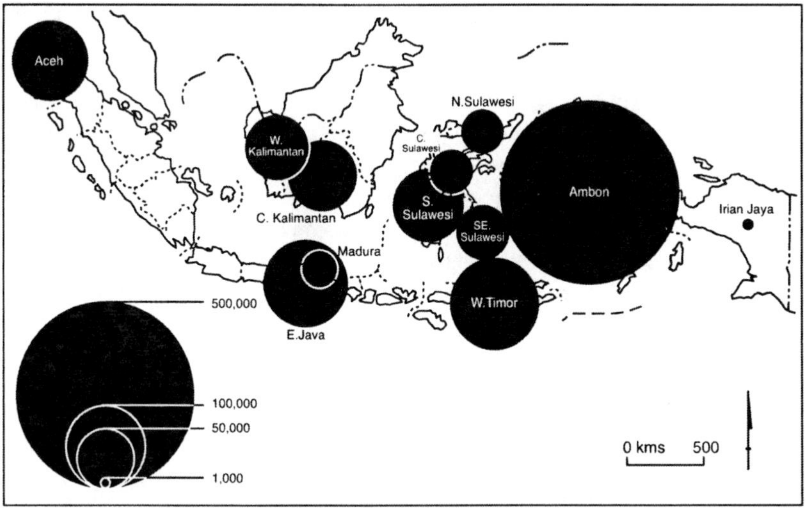

Source: Assembled from newspaper and magazine reports

International migration

Levels of international migration

One of the most substantial elements of globalisation processes that have been dominant in the last decade or so has been a parametric increase in the scale and complexity of mobility between nations. Indonesia of course has been massively influenced by international migration in its history, including during the colonial period, when not only the immigration of Dutch and other Europeans was crucial to the economic, social and political development of the archipelago, but also the associated immigration of Chinese and South Asian groups (Hugo 1980). During the first few decades of Independence Indonesia was not influenced much by international migration except for the repatriation of the Dutch and Chinese and the emigration of Moluccans (Hugo 1980). Since the 1990s, however, international migration has assumed much greater significance.

South–north migration

A distinctive feature of modern international migration is so called south–north migration involving a growing flow of more or less permanent migrants from Asia, Africa, Latin America, Oceania and the Middle East to the OECD countries. Indonesia has not participated in this as much as other Asian countries, as Table 8 indicates. However, this emigration from Indonesia is increasing. Table 9 shows the main OECD countries of destination and it is apparent that the largest community is in the Netherlands, reflecting the strong colonial linkages. The data in Table 8 and 9 only show the people who were born in Indonesia and not those of Indonesian origin, a number that could be several times larger. Hence, in the Netherlands it was reported that in 1998 the second generation Indonesian (Dutch-born with an Indonesian parent) population was 264,100.[3] The Moluccans are a significant group here and are predominantly descendents of the group, mainly from Ambon, who opted to go to the Netherlands with the returning Dutch on the proclamation of Indonesian independence.

The largest single destination of south–north migrants is the United States, although it has only the second largest overseas Indonesian community. The Indonesian-born community in Australia is growing rapidly—from 44,175 in 1996 to 61,700 in 2003. Skilled, educated groups are highly represented in south–north migration, raising the spectre of brain drain. Indonesians of Chinese ethnicity have been an important component of the emigration (Penny 1993), especially in the late 1990s, when there were anti-Chinese riots in Indonesia. There is a growing literature on diaspora suggesting that it can be a positive element in development of origin areas (Hugo 2003a).

An increasingly important element in global south–north migration is the movement of students from less developed countries to OECD nations. This overlaps with permanent migration, since a substantial number of the students remain at the destination after completing their studies and this process is being facilitated in some countries (Hugo 2006c). Figure 5 shows the growth of migration of Indonesian students to Australia.

Table 8: Number of Asia-born persons in OECD nations by country of birth, around 2000

Country of birth	Number now living in OECD countries
India	2,065,452
China	2,038,072
Philippines	2,035,897
Korea*	1,641,348
Vietnam	1,608,510
Pakistan	740,922
Japan	656,690
Hong Kong	643,190
Taiwan	457,957
Indonesia	349,276
Sri Lanka	329,893
Thailand	326,163
Bangladesh	312,303
Laos	276,953
Cambodia	248,044
Malaysia	230,482
Afghanistan	154,252
Singapore	121,061
Burma	63,876
Nepal	28,934
Macau	20,623
East Timor	11,723
Brunei	10,920
Mongolia	6,421
Bhutan	1,020
Maldives	580
Asia unspecified	412,016

Source: OECD
*Includes North Korea, South Korea and Korea unspecified

Table 9: Number of Indonesia-born persons in OECD nations around 2000

Country of residence	Number living in OECD countries
Netherlands	165,770
United States	75,370
Australia	47,158
Japan	14,610
Canada	10,660
Korea	10,513
United Kingdom	6,711
New Zealand	3,792
France	3,554
Belgium	2,754
Switzerland	2,410
Sweden	1,817
Austria	849
Spain	830
Norway	695
Denmark	639
Greece	261
Turkey	180
Ireland	157
Finland	133
Portugal	95
Czech Republic	88
Luxembourg	81
Mexico	70
Poland	44
Hungary	34
Slovakia	1
Germany	0
Total	349,276

Source: OECD

Figure 5: Australia: Indonesia-born student arrivals, 1991–92 to 2003–04

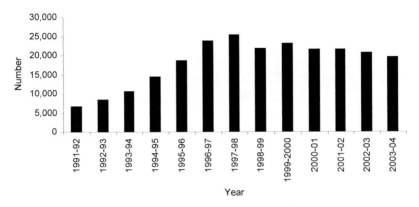

Source: DIMIA, various issues; DIMIA unpublished data

Labour migration

The largest international outflow from Indonesia has been of labour migrants—workers who work in overseas countries for a fixed period (usually two years) and then return. Figure 6 shows the numbers of workers being deployed overseas through the official system and demonstrates the substantial increase since the mid-1990s. An important shift has occurred in the last decade with the involvement of more Asian destinations, whereas in the early years of migration most official labour migrants went to the Middle East, mainly Saudi Arabia. This shift is evident in Table 10, which indicates the increasing importance of destinations like Malaysia, Singapore, Taiwan, Hong Kong, Brunei and South Korea as targets for Indonesian labour migrants. It is also to be noted in the table that women are dominant in most of the official labour migrant flows, so that they made up over two thirds of Indonesia's labour migrants. An associated official movement is that of 'trainees'—Indonesian workers in factories owned by Japanese or Korean companies who are transferred to the home country to undergo training at 'head office'. Table 11 shows the numbers involved. This type of migration has attracted controversy because they are often thinly disguised ways of recruiting workers for factories in Japan and South Korea that are experiencing difficulty in recruiting workers.

Figure 6: Number of Indonesian overseas workers processed by the Ministry of Manpower, 1979–2003

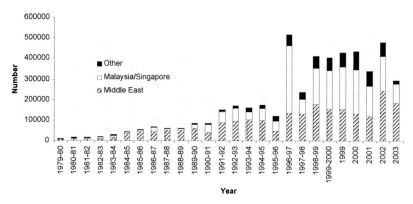

Sources: Suyono 1981; Singhanetra-Renard 1986:52; PPK 1986:2; Indonesian Department of Labour, unpublished data; DTK 1998:14; Soeprobo 2005.

Note: In 2000 the Indonesian government transferred to a calendar year system of accounting, having previously used 1 April–31 March.

Table 10: Indonesia: destinations of overseas workers, 1999–March 2004

Destination	Number	Percent	Sex ratio
Asia Pacific	1,163,366	56.6	72.2
Malaysia	733,493	35.7	105.6
Taiwan	156,258	7.6	28.3
Singapore	120,971	5.9	22.6
Hong Kong	83,299	4.1	16.9
South Korea	33,396	1.6	333.4
Brunei	26,270	1.3	48.9
Japan	8,886	0.4	446.5
Other Asia	901	0.0	4073.7
America	5,472	0.3	1853.6
Europe	2,183	0.1	1484.0
Middle East/Africa	885,682	43.1	16.0
Saudi Arabia	775,482	37.7	15.4
Arab Emirates	54,545	2.7	20.7
Other Middle East/Africa	55,655	2.7	15.9
Total	2,086,703	100.0	35.7

Source: DEPNAKER and Soeprobo 2005

Table 11: Indonesia: deployment of trainees to Japan and Korea, 1994–2003

	Japan	Korea
1994	2,984	na
1995	3,965	na
1996	5,098	na
1997	6,707	11,119
1998	5,972	8.363
1999	5,926	na
2000	6,231	na
2001	5,817	na
2002	4,925	na
2003	5,597	na

Sources: Iguchi 2000:22; 2005:21; SooBong 2000:13

It is important to appreciate that there is substantial undocumented labour migration that does not go through official channels in Indonesia. The official process has been expensive, time consuming and subject to corruption, and the government has recently attempted to reform the system. However, migrants often prefer undocumented migration because it is cheaper, faster and in some cases more reliable. There are three types:

• Migrants who clandestinely enter a country and do not pass through official border checkpoints. In Indonesia, for example, this includes large numbers who cross the Malacca Straits from Riau to the coasts of Johore in Malaysia.

• Migrants who enter a country legally but overstay their visa. This applies to many who enter Sabah from East Kalimantan.

• Migrants who enter a country under a non-working visa (such as an *umroh* or haj visa to enter Saudi Arabia, or a visiting pass to visit Sabah), but instead work in the destination country.

One of the largest undocumented flows, despite efforts to regularise the movement, has been to Malaysia; the main routes are shown in Figure 7. In recent years the Malaysian government has cracked down on this clandestine migration and expelled large numbers of undocumented Indonesian workers, but it is apparent that some sectors of the Malaysian economy are heavily reliant on Indonesian labour and may not be viable without access to that labour. It has been argued (Hugo 1993b) that Malaysian labour markets are segmented so that some areas (such as construction, plantations, domestic workers, forestry) have become dependent on cheap foreign labour and are eschewed by Malaysians even at times of economic downturn and high unemployment in Malaysia.

Figure 7: Major routes of undocumented migration from Indonesia to Malaysia

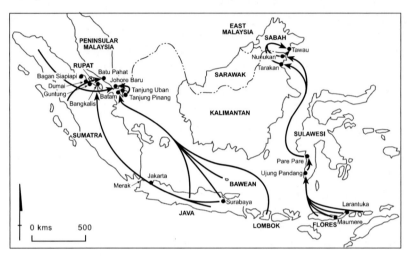

Source: Hugo 1998

Taking into account both documented and undocumented migration, Table 12 presents estimates of the contemporary stocks of labour migrants in the main receiving nations. It is extremely difficult to make these estimates because of the lack of data and the large scale of undocumented migration, but the table does indicate the significance of the migration. This significance is understated because the temporary nature of movement means there is a much greater number of people involved than the numbers in Table 12. Moreover the areas of origin of migrant workers are strongly geographically concentrated so the impact is magnified at the regional development level. Figure 8 shows that among official labour migrants, West Java is the main origin and it has been shown that it is particular areas within the province of West Java which are the main origins (Hugo 1998). Figure 9 shows the origins of undocumented migrant workers deported from Sabah and again a geographical concentration is in evidence.

Table 12: Estimated stocks of foreign labour in Asian countries around 2001

Country	Year	Stock	Source
Japan	2004	870,000	Iguchi 2005
South Korea	2004	423,597	Park 2005
Taiwan	2003	600,177	Lee 2005
Singapore	2004	580,000	Yap 2005
Malaysia	2004	1,359,500	Kanapathy 2005
Thailand	2004	1,623,776	Chalamwong 2005
Brunei	1999	91,800	*Migration News*, February 2000
Hong Kong	2003	216,863	Chiu 2005
Macau	2000	27,000	*Migration News*, September 2000
China	2003	90,000	Ma 2005
Vietnam	2001	30,000	Nguyen 2003
Indonesia	2004	91,736	Soeprobo 2005
Philippines	2003	9,168	Go 2005
Bhutan	2004	40,350	*Asian Migration News*, August 2004
Total		6,053,967	

Figure 8: Indonesia: province of origin of officially registered overseas workers, 1989–1992

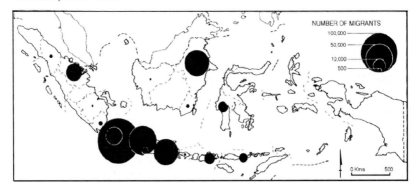

Source: Hugo 1998

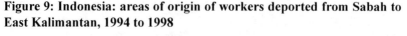

Figure 9: Indonesia: areas of origin of workers deported from Sabah to East Kalimantan, 1994 to 1998

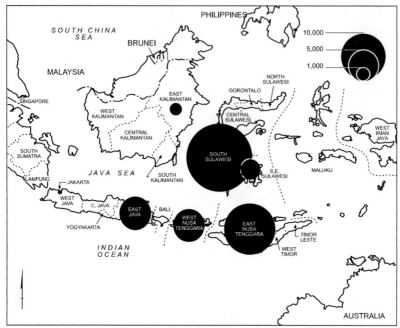

Source: Provincial Development Office of the province of East Kalimantan Samarinda

Indonesian labour migration, both official and undocumented, is overwhelmingly of unskilled labourers, despite efforts by the government to 'skill' the outflow. While women are dominant in the official outflow, men probably are the majority in the undocumented migration. Much of the recruitment of workers is undertaken by a complex set of agents who are important gatekeepers in both the official and undocumented migration systems. Protection of workers is an important issue and in the past Indonesia has not been as committed or as effective in protecting its workers overseas as countries like the Philippines (Hugo 2003b). Exploitation of workers occurs at all stages of the migration process—in recruitment, before departure, in the destination and on return. This can involve, before the migrants leave Indonesia, such practices as overcharging, not providing adequate preparation and training, employment by the agent before departure without remuneration, and agents recruiting people for non-existent jobs or not providing accurate information about the nature, conditions and wages of the overseas positions.

At the destination exploitation can take the form of overwork, underpayment, poor conditions and even physical or sexual abuse. On return official migrants must go through a dedicated airport terminal in Jakarta where they are subject to a set of charges—some of which are informal. It has been the case that many migrant workers are not given the necessary information and training before leaving to enable them to cope with exploitation at the destination. Moreover, the support systems, labour attaches and so on provided by the Indonesian government in destination countries are much more limited than is the case for the Philippines (Hugo 2003b). While undocumented migrants are at risk of exploitation in destinations because they lack official status, in some cases the fact that the move occurs through established national social networks means that the migrants have more (informal) support systems than is the case for official migrants.

Table 13: Studies of returned overseas contract workers: percent returning to Indonesia within one year

				Away less than one year	
Origin	Destination	Year	Reference	%	#
Central Java	Middle East	1986	Mantra, Kasnawi & Sukamardi 1986	18.1	167
Yogyakarta	Middle East	1986	Mantra, Kasnawi & Sukamardi 1986	63.4	93
West Java	Middle East	1986	Mantra, Kasnawi & Sukamardi 1986	21.0	100
West Java	Middle East	1992	Adi 1996	12.2	90
Java	Middle East	1999	Pujiastuti 2000	60.0	40
Java	Middle East/ Malaysia	1991	Spaan 1999	31.0	18

One important result of the problems with Indonesian official international migration outlined above is a very high rate of premature return among migrants. Table 13 shows findings from several surveys indicating a high proportion of labour migrants returning before their two year contract has expired. This can represent a substantial cost for the migrant workers and their families, since they often have to repay a loan taken out to fund the original migration and have not been away long enough to earn sufficient money to repay the loan. The vulnerability of overseas workers seems to be greater for women than men. This is partly a function of the majority of them being employed as domestic workers in private homes and lacking the protection available in other workplaces. There is an alarming rate of suicide and other deaths among Indonesian domestic workers abroad. It has been shown that the incidence of exploitation is almost non-existent among female labour migrants from Flores to Sabah, where women usually move with men and have networks of support in their destinations, compared with migration to the Middle East, where they are isolated from such support (Hugo 2003b).

Table 14: Survey village: reasons given by returned migrants for leaving the village

Level of satisfaction	Males		Females	
	#	%	#	%
Restricted opportunities in the village	74	81.3	24	70.6
Lack of funds	11	12.1	1	2.9
To help family	1	1.1	4	11.8
Family too restricted	2	2.2	4	11.8
Other	3	3.3	1	2.9
Total	91	100.0	34	100.0

It is apparent from field research that most labour migrants leave their home area because they perceive that they can earn much more at a foreign destination than they could at home. This is evident in Table 14, which shows results of a survey of returned migrants in Java about their reasons for leaving their village in the first place. These types of economic imperatives are duplicated in other surveys of migrants. The Indonesian government has encouraged international labour migration and given the following reasons for doing so:

• The inflow of remittances from migrant workers is an important source of scarce foreign exchange.

- The training and experience gained by migrant workers enhances the human resource base in Indonesia.

- The absorption of under-employed and unemployed workers in Indonesia.

However, it is difficult to estimate the size of the flow of remittances into Indonesia. The Bank of Indonesia uses a narrow definition of remittances as transfers represented by foreign banks. These exclude:

- money carried by return migrants,

- batching of remittances sent home with returning friends and relatives,

- in-kind remittances, such as appliances and gold,

- postal transfers, and

- company schemes to transfer remittances (Hugo 2005).

Figure 10: Growth of remittances to Indonesia, 1980 to 2002

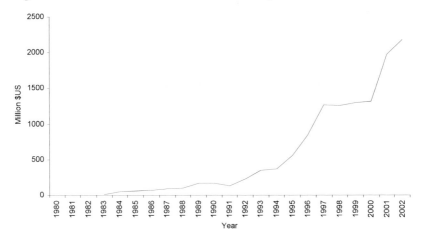

Source: IMF Balance of Payments Statistics Yearbooks; Soeprobo 2005

Nevertheless, Figure 10 shows that official remittance figures have increased substantially, although it indicates only the tip of the iceberg of actual flows. While official remittances only amount to only 2.1% of the value of exports (Hugo 2005), their impact is magnified at the regional and local levels. For example, West and East Nusa Tenggara are the poorest provinces in the nation, and remittances represent one of the few inflows of capital. In West Nusatenggara large numbers of workers have moved to palm oil plantations in Malaysia as the only way the escape the cycle of debt they face at home (*Indonesian Observer* 1995). From Malaysia those migrants sent home an amount larger than the entire provincial budget in 1995/96. Bank data from one district in East Nusatenggara found approximately US$1.5 million of remittances per year. The impact of remittances is felt most intimately by the poor in these provinces.

Conclusion

In the early years of the 21st century Indonesian migration is faced with a number of challenges. The 'push' from within Indonesia increased substantially following the economic and political crises in the late 1990s. Meanwhile the networks created by Indonesians who had moved overseas have proliferated, so that both labour migrants and permanent south–north migrants have flowed in increasing numbers. The migration industry in Indonesia has grown vigorously over recent decades, with agents and sub-agents now spread all over the country. Together, networks and the migration industry provide a strong element of momentum to Indonesian migration. On the other hand, in some destinations, there have been developments that have militated against Indonesian migrants. Most striking were the bans on Indonesian migrant workers imposed in Malaysia in the early years of the 21st century. These not only put a brake on migration but also saw many undocumented migrants captured, interviewed and deported, which created considerable hardship for them and their families. However, the reliance of important sectors of the Malaysian economy on migrant labour has seen an amelioration of that policy. There can be no doubt that there will continue to be a substantial demand for Indonesian international labour migrants for the foreseeable future.

The issues surrounding Indonesian labour migration, however, are not confined to labour markets and demand for labour. There has been substantial exploitation of Indonesian labour migrants and a lack of protection both at home and overseas. There have been increasing efforts to reform the system and provide protection for people working overseas and to prevent corruption and exploitation in the recruitment process. Undoubtedly the better preparation and training of workers is crucial. Non-government organisations have not been as involved in the protection and support of migrant workers as they have in other nations and need to be encouraged and given a central place in migrant worker protection.

With respect to south–north migration, it is likely too that the future will see an increase in outflows, although Indonesia has not as yet experienced the scale of emigration that several fellow ASEAN countries have recorded over the last decade. The significant outflow of students seeking tertiary education in OECD countries undoubtedly will see a significant proportion remain in those destinations after completion of their studies—although this has not been as big a problem as for other Asian nations. Indonesian diaspora are of significant size in a few OECD nations but are nothing like the scale of the Indian, Chinese, Filipino and Vietnamese expatriate communities. Nevertheless, there is scope in the future for Indonesia to develop expatriate, migration and development policies, and programs are now being considered by intermittent development agencies (Adams 2003; Ellerman 2003; Hugo 2003a; Asian Development Bank 2004; Martin 2004; Lucas 2004; House 2004; Newland 2004; Johnson & Sedacca 2004; IOM 2005).

There is no reason to believe that the increase in internal population mobility within Indonesia will not continue. The following would seem to be drivers that will see the scale and complexity of internal migration and circulation to continue:

- Marked spatial mismatches between sites of expanding job opportunity and the locations of potential workers.

- Rapid improvement in levels of education, resulting in young people in rural areas being unwilling to work in agriculture and moving to seek work in other sectors.

- Rapid commercialisation of the agricultural sector, replacing labour inputs with capital inputs.

- Strong cultural imperatives among some ethnic groups that encourage people to move out of the home area to seek work and experience.

- A strong tradition of people responding to local and regional conflict by moving on a temporary or permanent basis to work in other, more secure, areas.

- An entrenched pattern over much of Indonesia in which families seek to enhance their security by deploying some family members to work outside the home area to create multiple sources of income and reduce the effects on the family of the failure of one source of income.

- The proliferation of a 'migration industry' in Indonesia involving recruiters, travel providers, labour organisers and other intermediaries who facilitate the flow of labour to destinations within and outside the country.

- A tradition of families responding to crisis situations by sending out family members to destinations perceived to offer employment possibilities to send remittances to the home area.

Endnotes

1   For more comprehensive discussion of Indonesian internal and international migration data see Hugo (2000a) and Hugo (2000b) respectively.

2   These definitions have changed over time (Hugo 1993a).

3   Personal communication from Dr Philip J Muus.

Indonesians as Australians?

Janet Penny

The Indonesian-born population in Australia has never been a large one, considering the disparities in relative population sizes and standards of living in the two countries. Historically, the reasons are straightforward. Some are fundamentally political—the White Australia Policy, restrictions on movement placed by the Dutch colonial authorities, and Australia's identity as part of the British Empire. Further, because each country was a part of a different colonial empire there was a lack of knowledge by the people in each country of the other. In addition to political factors (and their close associates, economic factors), there are also cultural factors to be considered. Indonesia contains a variety of cultures that vary enormously in nature and complexity, as well as the size of their populations and their influence on the nation as a whole. Although some of these ethnic groups have a tradition of exploration and travel, overall the numerically and culturally dominant groups do not.

The Javanese, Sundanese and Balinese have traditionally regarded their home islands as sufficient unto themselves. Although population density has created economic scarcity sufficient to force emigration, the Javanese were reluctant, preferring to open up new land near their village of origin. When that was no longer possible, they participated in government-sponsored transmigration programs to other Indonesian islands. Many have also emigrated to other parts of Southeast Asia in search of work.

From Sumatra, Minangkabau and some Batak groups have historically been willing to travel, generally with the idea of returning—hopefully with enough wealth to establish themselves in the community with good standing. They maintained strong ties with their families, clans and place of origin during their sojourns abroad. Other groups from outer islands—Menadonese, Bugis and Makassarese, for example—have traditionally travelled in order to trade, maintaining their home base but staying away for some months each year. Some of these were in fact the first Indonesians to arrive in Australia, harvesting and preparing *trepang* for trade on Australia's northern coast from the late 17th century until early in the 20th century.

Since Independence in 1947, many Indonesians from all ethnic groups have already moved within their own country—from a village to town to study or work, or to a major city. A move to Australia can be seen in that context. My thesis, completed in 1993, was concerned with this one aspect of Indonesian mobility—migration to Australia between 1947 and 1986 (Penny 1993). In this paper I intend to re-visit the thesis from a different perspective, incorporating a study I did in the mid-1990s on mixed marriage, which included some examples of Indonesian-Australian families (Penny and Khoo 1996). I will concentrate on particular issues concerning this migration: family and cultural values, historical influences and their relation to migrants' long-term commitment to living in Australia.

Indonesians who have chosen to live in Australia have several advantages. The obvious one is that they are not very far away, physically, from their original home. The maintenance of ties is mainly dependent upon the cost of air fares and telephone calls. Thus, a move to Australia is an example of modern mobility, of which permanent migration is only one of several choices.

Most of the people I interviewed, both in the 1980s and 1990s, had moved within Indonesia more than once. Only 20 of those interviewed in the 1980s had not moved within Indonesia. Ten of these came from Jakarta, and the other ten had already lived overseas before coming to Australia. Another 20 had moved four or more times within Indonesia; the remaining 60 had moved consistently from villages to towns or from towns to cities. Some of the younger people had moved because their parents did; others moved to study or to work. All those I met in the 1990s for the intermarriage study echoed the patterns of the 100 interviewed for the thesis. Traditionally, the use of the term 'migration' for an international move implies a permanent decision, but for many of those interviewed the move to Australia was one of several options, and they were not at all certain of their long-term plans.

The degree of the migrants' previous mobility affected many aspects of their lives in Australia. For example, those who had moved most were those who used English most; they also were the most active participants in Indonesian cultural activities—music and the like—apparently not signifying a rejection of Australian life, but rather indicating a desire to maintain and display their culture to Australians. They were also the ones who were most sensitive to emotional and cultural misunderstandings between themselves and Australians. Those who had moved less described different concerns. For example they were very troubled by the inclination of their children to move away from the family home before they married. They too reported misunderstandings with Australians, but these usually involved language usage rather than feelings or more substantial problems. This suggested that their relations with Australians took a more superficial form.

Indonesian immigrants have, in addition to living near enough to Indonesia to travel and communicate easily, a further advantage. They have always lived in a multicultural society, so the notion of living alongside people with different first languages, different values and different cultural customs is by no means strange to them. Even so, the culture one is born into is a foundation against which new experiences are evaluated. Overseas migration shifts that foundation, and the migrant faces the difficult task of building a new one in the midst of the experiences themselves.

A third factor, and an important advantage, is that Indonesians' cultural history has made them accustomed to—and therefore skilled at—adaptation. For all its history, like many countries, Indonesia has been introduced to new religions, languages, art and cuisines. Indonesians have learned to take what they wish from each of the waves of religious influence—from Hinduism, Buddhism, Islam—each grafted on to varieties of animism practised in local cultures. Likewise, food, dance and music, art and clothing came to Indonesia from the main cultural streams through China, India and the Islamic Middle East. Then the whole package of Western European values and customs arrived during the colonial period and since Independence. While the element of choice may not have seemed obvious when the waves are washing over them (for example, Dutch colonialism), after enough time has passed, the elements that remain are those that best fit with the remnants of past waves, and with the original culture.

Religion has had an important influence on the adaptation of Indonesians to life in Australia. In 1986, while 87% of the population of Indonesia were Muslims, Muslims made up only 43% of the ethnic Indonesians living in Australia. And, while only 9% of Indonesia's population was Christian, in Australia 42% of ethnic Indonesians and 67% of ethnic Chinese Indonesian-born were Christians. (Of the remainder, 4% were Hindu—mostly from Bali—and 1% were Buddhists.) My survey showed that Indonesian Christians found that their religion was a factor in their relatively easy adjustment to Australian life. Protestants in particular found their churches to be a source of Australian friendships as well as an attachment to an Australian institution. Many of the Indonesian-born Chinese tended to become absorbed in the general Southeast Asian Chinese population, which made it easy to maintain religious practices.

Important changes in religious practice in Indonesia itself have taken place in the past two decades. The rise of Islamic piety has lent prestige to going on the Haj pilgrimage to Mecca, to the adoption of the *jilbab* scarf by Indonesian women and girls, and a heightened sense of difference from secular people or Christians. Preliminary investigations indicate that this may have caused Indonesians in Australia—depending on the intensity of their religious commitment—to reflect on the desirability of fitting in with Australians; or it may have affected their ability to feel comfortable in Australia, or conversely, in Indonesia should they wish to return. This question clearly needs further examination.

People's responses to these elements—values, religion and changes in location and in behaviour have varied, of course. Sets of cultural values that came to Indonesia over the centuries became absorbed into the Indonesian character. They contrasted with values and behaviour the migrants have found in Australia, where Indonesians have had to deal with three principal issues:

1. Indonesian—particularly Javanese—emphasis on social harmony (with its attendant possibility of dishonesty) contrasts with Australians' value for candour (with the disadvantage of seeming to Indonesians to be bluntness shading into rudeness). Many have tried to combine the two, aiming to have smooth and pleasant social relations and yet prevent misunderstandings through lack of candour, while avoiding Australian bluntness, which makes Indonesians distinctly uncomfortable.

2. Certainties and stability are implied in an ordered social hierarchy (which can lead to social rigidities and—in Australian eyes—to unfairness) versus Australia's relative disorder, which can lead to social mobility, individual equality and relative political freedom. Indonesians can see this as leading to uncertainty. Many Indonesians have managed to combine the best of both, particularly within the family, where respect for the aged can be combined with personal independence.

3. Mutual support networks are seen as useful—even as a cultural ideal, expressed as *gotong royong*—particularly when migrants are cut off from traditional supports of family, but many complained that they also involved judgmental gossip and the need to conform. Without them, however, isolation could be a problem, so the Australian value for individual freedom had its costs, too. This particular set of values has come to seem less specific to the Indonesian-Australian experience than to migrants in general. Indonesians who came from large cities, or who had not lived in the area of their ethnic background, already experienced this in Indonesia. It is probably fair to say that Australians who move from small to large communities have similar experiences.

These values illustrate the cultural foundation that is part of the immigrants' baggage, along with the contrasting values that are part of the new landscape that they must negotiate. Whether or not they do so to their (and their family's) satisfaction will influence their whole experience in Australia, and thus the commitment to the migration.

In addition to the contrasting values, there are more obvious adjustments to be made—food, drink and clothing. These changes are relatively easy to adopt, and choices are consciously and freely made. In recent years the ingredients for Indonesian food have been easy to find. Having Indonesian food only in the evening and at times of celebration is a common response to the lack of help and relative lack of time; another is the use of convenience foods mixed with traditional cooking. Adjusting to Australian drinking of alcohol was a problem for some of those I talked to, and solutions varied with age groups and religious beliefs.

Requirements for immigrants to speak English are a major element in their admission to Australia, but the experience of Indonesians raises real questions about its relevance. Most Indonesians know a number of languages, whether or not they have had higher education—the language of their ethnic group plus Indonesian are basic. Early immigrants (all with some education) knew Dutch. The very mobility of modern Indonesia has meant for instance that many learn the Jakarta dialect as well as a smattering of another local language.

Of course it is vital to speak and understand English easily (if not altogether 'correctly') if social and cultural integration is to take place. But the relationship between good English on arrival and eventual mastery of English as a social and cultural tool is not direct. About half the respondents had arrived with what they considered poor English, and while higher education was an advantage in the beginning, after some time it was not as influential as was familiarity with several languages. For example, a few informants had been sea-farers, learning some of several languages, and they found adding English less difficult than the few who had only known their ethnic language and Indonesian. Marriage to a non-Indonesian was naturally a strong incentive to learn English, but I also met mixed families where the Australian partner used considerable Indonesian.

For many of the Indonesian cultural groups, marriage patterns are so similar to Western ones that they are not a bar to integration. In *Intermarriage* we found that over time the divorce rate in Indonesia has fallen. Because young people are educated longer and resist arranged marriages, they increasingly choose for themselves. The Australian divorce rate was increasing at that same time, due to increased freedom from family pressure. The result is that the divorce rates for Indonesians and Australians quite coincidentally converged at around 40%.

Indonesia is unusual among immigrant homelands, particularly Asian ones: women traditionally have been able to work outside the home, and men have been involved in raising the children. The main block to a woman's choice to join the paid workforce once they are in Australia has been lack of extended family members to help with the household. Thus the role of women in Indonesia is so similar to Australian patterns there is no real culture clash.

To sum up, differences in cultural style—in religious practices, in behaviour, in language and in family values and practices—all must be negotiated, and as migrants go through this process, they make a range of choices. The traditional model of migrant assimilation is a straight line, from the decision to migrate, through the processes of arrival and physical and emotional settlement, to final assimilation. However, as reported by those interviewed in my research, the actual experience is much more complex. The model on the following page comes closer to describing the actual range of choices faced by migrants:

This model shows that some choose not to adopt Australian customs and values, either returning to Indonesia or becoming absorbed in the Indonesian expatriate community. Some migrants plan that the time spent in Australia is intended to be solely to enable them to return in a more prosperous position. Therefore they adopt external behaviour which favours this, particularly in the workplace, and if successful, they do achieve their aims and return to Indonesia. There are also some who wholly adopt Australian ways, and rarely mix with other Indonesians and rarely return to Indonesia. Between these extremes on the continuum are those who combine the behaviour and values of both cultures, remaining at a midway point on the diagram opposite. This was a goal frequently mentioned during the interviews for the thesis in the 1980s. In the *Intermarriage* study, of the six migrant groups studied (American, Dutch, Italian, Lebanese, Indonesian, Chinese), Indonesians were the cultural group most likely to consciously choose this option, and also the most likely to succeed.

A number of factors influence this process:

- the intentions of the migrants when they first decide to come;

- the migrants' circumstances before leaving (the size, prosperity and attitudes of their family, their age, their economic prospects or wealth or lack of it, education and social standing.) The attitudes of their family towards the migration also plays some part in their decisions;

- the triggering factors that set them on their way (a personal opportunity or a crisis, the general state of the nation and its expanding or limiting of opportunities, an invitation to come to Australia for a particular reason—for instance a job, a scholarship, a love affair, or a relative living here);

- the welcome in Australia (from friends or family, success in educational or work experience, and ability to speak English within a reasonable time);

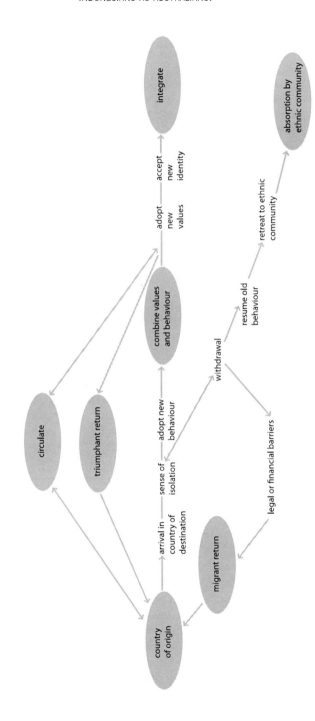

Indonesians as Australians: model of migrant agency and potential outcomes

- continuing circumstances at home (family matters, the economic choices etc.);

- the way life develops in Australia. Sometimes personal developments determine choices, as when migrants' children who are born in Australia are clearly more attached to Australia than to Indonesia. The ties of migrants to Indonesia may also become looser, as for example when migrants' parents pass away, or if it becomes difficult to afford to return, or to circulate as one might wish.

And all these factors are affected by the individual characteristics of the migrant himself or herself—intelligence, likeability, and most of all, adaptability.

Each of these factors justify our attention, but this paper focuses on the historical influences on the nature of this migration.

Historical influences

Those who first came to Australia after Indonesia's independence, from 1947, were intended by the then 'white Australia' to be temporary. A large proportion of those who came in the 1950s and early 60s expected to return after a few years. They were eager to become educated in order to contribute to the development of their new nation. Many studied engineering, as at that time educational opportunities—particularly in technical fields—were very limited in Indonesia. Those not studying were mainly broadcasters or language teachers. But those who found themselves holding satisfactory jobs, or were married to Australians, or were simply members of families who had made Australia their home, preferred to remain in Australia. Some of those who came in the early years eventually found that their job prospects were limited to 'being Indonesian', that is, they had been invited for that reason to teach Indonesian history or language, and some felt trapped in a kind of professional ghetto.

By the 1970s economic circumstances in Indonesia enabled people from a wider range of skills and qualifications to gather the money to travel, and to consider moving abroad. A much stronger Indonesian economy, increasing information about foreign lands, along with a pent-up demand for wider experience, combined to send many curious or ambitious people to move abroad. A larger migration was the result—about 5000 during the 1970s—among whom were a considerable proportion of young people who interrupted their studies, either through failure or indecision about goals, to travel and try a new place. By this time the 'white Australia policy' had been abandoned in law and practice, and new migrants from Indonesia were accepted. Their occupations ranged more widely, with many taking blue collar jobs. At the same time, this larger Asian immigrant population included refugees from Indochina, and their presence raised other issues. One result was to re-ignite a degree of Australian racism. This refugee influx was clear evidence that Australia *is* in Asia, and it made some Australians uneasy, or even hostile.

To most Australians all Asians were perceived as the same. The Indonesians who had arrived in the 1950s and 1960s had been well educated—in general even more than the general Australian population—but the refugees were not, nor were some of the new Indonesian migrants. Indonesians who had already settled in Australia had lost their sense of being considered a special, well respected category.

During the 1980s the pattern altered again, this time because the Australian admissions requirements became tighter, and immigrants had to meet economic criteria to gain visas. A higher proportion of young families came, one member of whom was likely to hold some kind of trade certificate, such as a diploma in banking, or secretarial work. Education in Indonesia had by this time improved greatly, with English widely taught and specialised training courses developed, enabling more Indonesians to meet immigration criteria. Also, Australians by this time travelled frequently to Indonesia, just as many Indonesians visited Australia as tourists, or to visit friends and relations who had settled here. One inevitable outcome of these interchanges has been increased intermarriage.

During the 1990s these patterns appear to have continued. However, the decision by the Bureau of Statistics not to ask questions about ancestry on census forms until 2001 has made it impossible to be precise about what proportion of the Indonesian-born are ethnic Indonesians, East Timorese, ethnic Chinese, Dutch colonials, Vietnamese born in transit camps, or 'others'. In the 1986 census these were significant percentages, with only 31% of all the Indonesian-born claiming 'Indonesian' ethnicity. Subsequently, the East Timorese were included in the overall total, further complicating the statistical picture. Without these separate ethnic categories cross-tabulated against economic and social indicators, generalisations about the nature of the immigrants and their integration are not possible until the data from the 2001 census are thoroughly analysed.

It was clear from my interviews that national as well as personal factors influenced both migration and integration. Since then changes—whether positive or negative—in the politics of both countries have impacted on Indonesians' sense of well-being and security in both places.

In Indonesia, the fall of the Soeharto government and the subsequent series of political and economic changes had some effect on Indonesians in Australia, but it was, according to informants, marginal. People were settled here, and it would not have affected the plans of more than a very few, who might want to go back to try to reestablish a business. It was also suggested that people may have felt that corruption will end and it will again be easier to establish a successful business. Most, however, felt glad to be in Australia and avoid the confusion and possible chaos and breakdown that might occur during that politically unsettled time. My informants reported that they were pleased to see, on the other hand, that the greater freedom since Soeharto's rule ended has meant that the media is now much more open, and people have better access to information than they did during Soeharto's time.

With regard to Chinese-Indonesian immigrants, however, the changes in train since the end of Soeharto's rule may have increased their sense of uncertainty, and strengthened their decision to stay in Australia.

The rise of fundamentalist Islam in recent years has been demonstrated by the increase in mosques, and pressure on women to wear the *jilbab*, and aggressive missionary actions: this has made it harder on what Indonesians sometimes call 'cultural' or 'statistical' Moslems as well as on Christians. Among some Indonesians in Australia this contributes to concern for family members back home. These issues are not static within Indonesia. For example, the prevalence of the *jilbab* reached a high point a few years ago, but is reportedly slightly less obvious recently.

In Australia, two events served to show that there is still a vein of prejudice in Australia that can be tapped. The rise of Pauline Hanson was the first of these, and while it was short-lived, it succeeded in making Indonesians feel somewhat uneasy about their relations with Australians. According to some informants, still more telling was the success of the Liberals in winning the election by tapping that vein by allowing stories of refugee behaviour to colour Australians' perceptions of 'the others'. The effect was even stronger in Indonesia than here, and fed into the wishes of some to paint Australia as anti-Islam and hostile to Indonesia.

September 11 and its aftermath must also be considered a factor in the decision-making process of Indonesians in Australia and those who might consider migrating.

The rise in militant Islam may well affect the choices made by Chinese, by Christians, and by some of the moderate, tolerant (traditional Indonesian) Muslims as well. Conversely, Australians' uneasiness about the influence of Islam may contribute to the migrants' decisions.

Future plans

Edward Said has said that: 'Migrancy and exile involve a discontinuous state of being...[and they are transformed] into a potent, even enriching motif of modern culture' (Chambers 1994:2). Homes are provisional, implying a strong sense of loss which exists alongside the sense of gain when a new home has been chosen. As with all migrants, the conflict between sets of ties affects the commitment of Indonesians living in Australia. The responses of those whom I interviewed in 1985 indicated that modern population movements such as this one are not so much migrations in the traditional sense, as they are examples of modern mobility. With changes in the availability of information about distant places, and with accessible transportation people move from one country to another for a variety of reasons, and with a variety of outcomes. With relatively cheaper air fares, it is possible for parents and children to live in either country and still keep in close contact. This enables people to circulate between the countries more freely than in the past.

Immigration is the first step; adjustment and integration with the host country is the next, and there are three aspects to the integration process— economic, social and cultural. Whether to stay on to the end of one's life is the third stage, and as earlier shown diagramatically there are three possibilities: to stay, to return or to circulate. There is often a very loose correlation between those who come to Australia with the intention of staying permanently and those who wanted to stay at the time of the interviews. In my sample of 100, it was about half of each—but not the same half.

Many Indonesian residents of Australia say they dream of returning 'home' to retire. The statistics show what proportion of those calling themselves 'settlers' actually did return. (Published data are only available after 1974, when the number was large enough to be included). Between 1975 and 1979 between 13% and 23% of Indonesia-born departures were settlers returning. In the years from 1980 through 1998 the average of those departures dropped to 6%.

Among the 100 Indonesians interviewed in the mid-1980s, the relationship between original intentions to stay permanently and intentions at the time of the interviews was surprisingly loose. About half had intended to stay, and half of those had changed their intentions; of those, seven (who had married Australians) hoped to circulate equally between the two countries. Another ten would have preferred to retire in Indonesia, but felt their family or economic circumstances would not permit it. The most common reason for changing their minds was the sense that their careers were limited, either to jobs with low language requirements or they were in occupational ghettos. On the other hand, of thirty who had only come for a temporary stay, eight had decided to make it permanent, mainly because of good job satisfaction.

Patterns of commitment tended to be influenced by the circumstances of the move. Those who came early, in the 1950s, to study or work, expected to return home, and most did that. Those who stayed were the exception, usually because they married Australians. Of those who came later during the 1960s, and during the 1980s, about 60% planned to stay permanently. The particular group who came during the 1970s were, in large part, adventurous young men, who planned to see the world, hopefully make some money and return home to settle down. In this group ten years on, less than half planned to settle in Australia. This may be partly attributable to their youth, as they were still at an age to make open-ended plans. It is not surprising, then, that the highest proportion of 'settlers' returning home was during the 1970s. By the 1980s people had considerable information about life here before they came, so their intentions were more firmly fixed.

Those who had been longest in Australia found that, as they aged, they were increasingly drawn to spend more time in Indonesia, and although their partners were not committed to returning, they said they were open-minded about it. The more recent arrivals varied. Those whose families had been very mobile within Indonesia, and were as a consequence fragmented—some even dysfunctional—had little wish to return. Some young women who were at home with small children missed the communal life and companionship they imagined they would have had in Indonesia, and dreamed of returning.

In analysing the data with regard to long-term commitment to staying in Australia, a number of variables were considered. Ethnicity was one. Different ethnic groups expressed different intentions in this regard: the majority of Chinese, Sundanese and Batak intended to stay permanently; around half of the Javanese and other smaller groups planned to stay. The Balinese were reluctant to commit themselves, as were those from other outer islands.

Education is a variable that presents a confused picture. Four-fifths of those who held post graduate qualifications on arrival were dissatisfied with their prospects in Australia and wanted to return. In the 1980s it appeared that job prospects in Indonesia looked better, and they felt that they would be able to afford a higher standard of living there. Just over half of the twenty-three who held Bachelor of Arts degrees had originally intended to stay; by 1987 only eight were still pleased with their decision to migrate. They also suspected that they would do better if they returned.

Most of those who were part way through university studies had not come with clear-cut intentions to stay anyway, and they continued to be undecided.

Those eighteen who held specific vocational qualifications comprised the single most explanatory variable: sixteen of them were pleased with their decision to migrate, which had been carefully taken, based on good information about job prospects. The kinds of vocational training most often mentioned were in white-collar areas—banking, secretarial and business work.

Seventeen respondents had completed high school, but had no further formal education. Of those, five felt that their situation in Indonesia had been unpromising, and had improved their prospects in Australia, while five felt they were worse off in Australia. Most of these planned to return to Indonesia or circulate. Nine out of the fourteen who had not completed high school planned to stay in Australia. Most of these were women who had followed their husbands.

Socio-economic status (SES) is a also complex variable. In Indonesia, as in Australia, it is based on access to resources; in both countries this is most directly determined by family status, which automatically provides access to money and education. In both countries it is also possible to overcome some level of disadvantage through education.

In general, if immigrants lowered their socio-economic status after arrival, they were more likely to wish to return; a corollary of this is that economic resources may make a 'successful' return difficult. Of those who came from lower SES in Indonesia, about a quarter planned to stay, and they were the same people who had come with little knowledge of Australia's economic prospects. All who had raised their SES hoped to return to Indonesia if they could afford to retire there, and none identified themselves as Australians. Those who either maintained the same status or who had lost status had a wide range of degrees of attachment to Australia. Most of those from the lower strata in Indonesia who were from cities had little attachment to Indonesia, and planned to stay in Australia. However, those from rural areas fully expected to return, as 'home' was clearly their village.

The length of time planning the move proved to be the best predictor of long-term commitment to staying in Australia. At the time of the interviews, 64% of those who had planned their migration for years, 50% of those who had planned the migration for several months, and only 27% of those who planned for only a few weeks, still planned to stay permanently in Australia.

Migrants' motives in coming to Australia were also a good indicator of long-term intentions, although not as closely correlated as the planning time. Those who came to marry or to a particular job were more likely to plan permanent migration overall. Those who came for 'personal' reasons—to join a family member, to follow a spouse were the least committed to stay, as their commitment was almost entirely dependent on their relationship with others. Those who came just to have an adventure were, at the time of the interviews, not at all sure they wanted to stay permanently in Australia. On the other hand, those who came for their own or their children's education, intending to stay, maintained their intentions.

When asked whether they 'felt like an Australian', the Indonesians interviewed gave answers that ranged from regarding the question as an absurdity to those who enthusiastically considered that they did indeed. The twenty-eight who thought the idea absurd included all those who came to join their children, and most of the older Indonesians. Most of them followed one of the Eastern religions, but other than that they ranged across ethno-linguistic groups, socio-economic classes and marital categories. Those ten who did feel Australian included those from mixed ethnicity within Indonesia, some Chinese, and some from outer islands. Nearly all of these planned to retire in Australia. In between were some who thought they might eventually feel Australian, or surely their children would, and others who believed they could develop a combined identity incorporating the best of both cultures and values.

My knowledge of the long-term integration of those arriving in the 1990s and since is much less detailed, unfortunately. Those interviewed for the intermarriage study were not representative of the population as a whole, since they were, of course, married to Australians. There were only eight Indonesians interviewed, but although they cannot be considered representative of any population, they do illustrate a range of possibilities. While the 1970s and 1980s were characterised by stable, generally good relations between the two countries, events in the 1990s and 2000s—Australia's role in the independence of East Timor and responses to changes in Indonesia's governments—have destabilised the relationship. The impact of this change would need a separate study to show their impact on the whole process of migration and integration between the two countries.

Finally, I would like to close with a quote from *The book of embraces*, by Uruguayan novelist Eduardo Galeano: 'Identity is no museum piece sitting stock-still in a display case, but rather the endlessly astonishing synthesis of the contradictions of everyday life' (in Rumbaut 1997:954).

Butonese in the Banda Islands: departure, mobility and identification

Phillip Winn

'Indonesia, and indeed the whole island world of Nusantara, presents a vast
historical panorama of displacement' (Fox 2001:68).

In any historically informed discussion of population displacements in
Indonesia, the Banda Islands must occupy a prominent place. The main
source of nutmeg and mace in the fabled 'spice islands' of the Moluccas and
an important regional trading centre during the pre-colonial period, this tiny
group of islands was conquered by the Dutch East India Company (or VOC)
in 1621.¹ The direct result was the expulsion of nearly the entire population
of some 13–15,000 people. The Bandanese could be said to be among the first
of the colonially displaced populations of the Indonesian archipelago, and the
memory of this event continues to reverberate not just in the islands themselves
but throughout the region (Fox 2001:69).

In this chapter I will focus on just one aspect of the complex repercussions of
this historical event—not the displacement of the exiled Bandanese, but rather
their replacement by other incoming peoples. The islands were repopulated over
several centuries under Dutch rule, which aimed at controlling production and
trade in local spices. The new arrivals included slaves, convicts, indentured or
contract ('coolie') labour and freely arriving in-migrants. I focus here on those
contemporary inhabitants who acknowledge ancestral origins in the Tukang
Besi Islands, located immediately to the southeast of Sulawesi. Known in
the islands as Butonese (in the local Malay: *orang Butung*), they formed a
substantial segment, some 20–30%, of the population of the Bandas in 1999
(which had once again reached around 15,000). Butonese are renowned both
as a highly mobile and highly dispersed population, particularly in eastern
Indonesia where they have established a significant permanent presence
across numerous locations. However, they remain understudied and poorly
understood.

My intention here is twofold. Firstly, to provide some insight into
conceptions of the Buton 'homeland' among Butonese who have been settled
for some generations in the Banda Islands. My assertion is a straightforward
one: that the socio-economic circumstances of their out-migrating ancestors
have had an important effect on these contemporary Butonese in terms of their
narratives of homeland, and thence on their attachment to the Banda Islands
as a place. Such a premise concurs with Fox (2001:67) when he suggests

that 'displacement must always begin with a departure…the departure itself
may affect—temper, inform and possibly determine—the new placement'.
Specifically, those Butonese whose ancestors are represented as fleeing
the onerous burdens of a system of social rank are more likely to distance
themselves from being Butonese and to engage in activities defining of
Bandanese identity.

Secondly, following on from this, I want to reflect briefly on notions of
diaspora in comparison with the Malay–Indonesian discourse of *merantau*.
In particular, I suggest that *merantau* is better suited to taking account of
the multiple meanings of departure that are able to give rise not only to
displacement, but also, and as importantly, (re)emplacement.The discussion
draws on ethnographic research in the Banda Islands over 1996-1997 and in
1999 carried out under the auspices of the Indonesian Institute of Sciences
(*Lembaga Ilmu Pengetahuan Indonesia*). This research explored the dynamics
of identification and sociality in the islands (see Winn 2002).

Who are the Butonese?

Of Southern Sulawesi's maritime peoples, sometimes referred to by the
initialism BBM—Bugis, Butonese and Makassarese—, the Butonese have been
called 'the most difficult to define' (Fox 1995:viii). The problematic of Butonese
identity highlights the frequent over-reliance within discourses of ethnicity on
ideas of static and bounded linguistic–territorial entities. In embracing some
14 different languages and more than a dozen islands, the notion of Butonese
identity violates any such assumptions. As a result, the expression frequently
attracts inverted commas, as does Buton itself as a place of origin.

The term Buton is certainly capable of carrying multiple meanings. It can
refer to a single island within the Indonesian province of Southeast Sulawesi.
It is also the name of a *kabupaten*, that is, a regency or district, a level of
local government immediately below that of the province. The administrative
boundaries of *kabupaten* Buton include a southern section of both Buton and
Muna Islands, along with a small group of islands to their southeast called the
Tukang Besi (or Tukangbesi) Islands. This boundary relates to a third sense of
the term—the historical realm known as the Sultanate of Buton, which at one
time embraced a much larger area than the contemporary *kabupaten*, taking
in the whole of Buton and Muna Islands, for example. The formation of this
realm was the achievement of a local ruling dynasty called Wolio, centred on
the southwest of Buton Island.

Dutch colonial strategies aiming at controlling trading activities not only
displaced populations but also shaped processes of socio-political representation.

In the Sulawesi–Maluku trading region the Dutch sought to create a strategic buffer between its two most powerful kingdoms—Makassar (in Sulawesi) and Ternate (in Maluku). To this end, the VOC signed an agreement with the ruler of Wolio in 1613 agreeing to defend his realm against their incursions (Fox 1995:ix). Through this alliance the VOC actively determined (and helped enforce) the extent of Wolio's claims to sovereignty. Here as elsewhere Dutch treaties of contract with different rulers in the archipelago worked to establish the identification of persons as subjects of a particular 'allegiance group', so that individuals and populations became identifiable in terms of rulers and, by extension, the 'place' of the ruler (Fox 2001:71). Notions of Buton and the Butonese were born in the crucible of colonial ethnicising nomenclature, with the Wolio language established as the administrative language of the Buton sultanate.

Before discussing the Butonese in the Bandas, it is crucial to appreciate the place of the Tukang Besi Islands within the Buton realm. There are four main islands in the Tukang Besi chain: Wanci (sometimes Wancé), Kaledupa, Tomia (Tomea) and Binongko. These islands were absorbed into the Buton sultanate in 1667 in a treaty witnessed by the then Dutch ally, the Sultan of Ternate, who abandoned all historical claims to the same area. At this time the Tukang Besi population had become increasingly aligned with the major Dutch enemy–competitor in the region, Makassar. Indeed, following the treaty, a number of revolts forced the Sultan of Buton to relocate a group of Cia-Cia speakers from the south of Buton Island to Binongko in order to secure its allegiance to the Buton realm; Cia-Cia speakers remain there today. As a result of this treaty, the population of the Tukang Besi Islands has been described as falling within the 'cultural dominion' of the sultanate of Wolio. The sultan appointed a local ruler, the *Meantu'u* based at Lia, on Wanci Island (Donohue 1995:3). A contemporary commentator notes that the islands 'generally acknowledge and take pride in the sultan, though notably less so than the mainland peoples on Buton [Island itself]' (Donohue 1995:3).

The Tukang Besi Islands have played a prominent part in the general characterisation of the Butonese as one of the most mobile populations in eastern Indonesia. In 1987, of the total 1,281 local trading vessels (known as *perahu lambo*) recorded in the *kabupaten*, 46% were based in the Tukang Besi Islands. Such figures continue a longstanding pattern. In 1919 a Dutch military estimate suggested some 300 *perahu* were present in 'the country of Buton', 200 of which were in the Tukang Besi Islands, and half of these in Binongko (Southon 1995:16). It is important to note that, as Dutch knowledge concerning the intricacies of local political cultures increased, more specific identifiers appeared, though often inconsistently applied (Fox 2001:71). The strategic significance of Binongko both as a site of early rebellion against the Buton sultanate and as a centre of local shipping probably explains why its name sometimes appears as distinct from Buton, certainly much more regularly than the other islands of the Tukang Besi group.

The Tukang Besi Islands are also renowned as a source of out-migration. Authors generally account for this in ecological terms: poor soils, scarce water and 'barely viable agriculture' (Southon 1995:17) force the population to seek a living through other occupations, such as maritime trading, or to leave the islands. This is a plausible explanation: Binongko is reputed to have the worst soils and the poorest fishing grounds, explaining its possession of the greatest fleet of ships and the highest level of out-migration.[2] The latter is so marked that one researcher suggests: 'Tukang Besi communities with permanent residents on islands in eastern Indonesia tend to be descended from Binongko traders' (Donohue 1995:4). There are settlements throughout eastern Indonesia that bear the name 'Binongko' (Fox 1995:ix), while in the province of Nusa Tenggara Timur in particular the expression 'Binongko' often appears synonymous with that of 'Buton' (Grimes et al. 1997:11). Grimes et al. (1997:11) go on to state that 'among these multiethnic communities speaking a variety of languages, the Wolio language is occasionally still used as a language of interethnic communication and to emphasise the solidarity of the "Buton" identity'.

The significance of the inverted commas appearing here around the term 'Buton' is unclear. It may simply reflect the multiple meanings of the noun itself as described previously—island, sultanate and district. However, applied here in the context of ethnic identity, there is the risk of an implication that Buton identity should itself be regarded as dubious, as if the 'multiethnic' character of the populations espousing such an identity, self-evident in the presence of more than one language, somehow undermines their claim to a shared, singular identification. Such a view would invoke the long-established conceptual nexus of language–territory–identity so fundamental to historical projects of representing ethnic groups and nations. Similar assertions have raised thorny questions within theories of ethnicity in the social sciences. Forth (1994) observes that the core problem frequently reduces to a quandary of whether use of an ethnonym is best based on objective or subjective criteria. This difficulty goes to the heart of the categorising impulse that has characterised aspects of anthropological endeavour and calls into question the discipline's relation to the epistemology of the natural sciences.

A far more productive orientation to forms of collective identification, and one that has come to overshadow other approaches in the social sciences, involves an appreciation of the situated and often strategic dimensions within representations of difference and commonality. In this approach, visions of discretely bounded 'ethnic groups' possessing sets of distinctive cultural traits have tended to give way to detailed examinations of particular contexts of identification (cf. Norval 1996). The social processes that emerge are far more dynamic and nuanced than a presumptive stress on shared and contiguous territory and language would allow. Ideas of 'being Butonese' then, as held by the descendants of out-migrants from the Buton region, may well not be limited to, or even concerned with, issues of linguistic uniformity. Fox (1995:ix) has pointed to socio-political and historical factors underpinning contemporary expressions of Butonese identity: 'determined by their own traditions, the Butonese are the peoples of the islands that once constituted the realm of the Sultan of Buton'. In the Bandas, a significant proportion of those who identify as *orang Buton* emphasise ancestral links to the *kabupaten* as much, if not more than, the Buton sultanate. A key factor appears to be the envisaged status of one's ancestors in the social system associated with the sultan.

Butonese in the Banda Islands

All of those identified and/or identifying as Butonese (*orang Butung*) in the Bandas acknowledge having ancestral links to the Tukang Besi Islands and each of these islands was represented among those tracing such a connection. As a result, Binongko was not used as a synonym for Buton. When the issue of specific origins in the Buton region was pressed, the acronym 'Wakatobi' tended to be offered, which combined the initial two letters of the names of each of the Tukang Besi Islands—Wanci–Kaledupa–Tomia–Binongko. This term did not compete with identification as Butonese, but existed as a physical locale encompassed by the Butonese ethnic group (*suku bangsa Butung*), a point explicitly rendered in formulations such as *Butung-Wakatobi*. Similarly, individual islands, when elicited, were given secondary status—*Butung-Tomia* or *Butung-Wanci*, for example. Differences between the islands of Tukang Besi were always minimised.

Tukang Besi languages were used, rather than Wolio, and were referred to ubiquitously as Butonese (*bahasa Butung*). While the several languages spoken in Tukang Besi were acknowledged as having distinct features, they were generally viewed as fundamentally alike.[3] In fact *bahasa Butung* in use in the Bandas often consisted of a fluid, near-situational process described by the people involved as '*baku cari bahasa*' ('finding a language together').[4] This involved two interlocutors drawing on and modifying their respective Tukang Besi linguistic resources in order to arrive at a form of speaking *bahasa Butung* that was mutually intelligible. For some, particularly younger generations, a somewhat standardised form of *bahasa Butung* was used, probably based on this situational process and perhaps forming an example of pidgin Tukang Besi described by Donohue (1995:1) as occurring elsewhere in eastern Indonesia. *Bahasa Butung* was the only form of non-Malay language widely in use in the Banda Islands.

To unravel the complexity of Butonese identity and its operation in the Bandas it would be necessary to explore the nature of interactions between the non-Butonese majority and the Butonese minority populations. Such is not the task of this chapter. Here I wish to highlight just two features referred to both by Butonese and non-Butonese informants as marking *orang Butung*: an ability to speak Butonese and a name prefix—*La* for men and *Wa* for women (eg La Salé, Wa Hamida).[5] Both features were waning, a circumstance that doubtless contributed to their status as especially defining of Butonese identity, where present. *Bahasa Butung* (in whatever form) was being replaced as the first language of individuals and households by local Malay, while the distinguishing name prefix was being abandoned altogether. Importantly, the degree to which this process was occurring differentiated the Butonese population of the Bandas into two segments. It was markedly more obvious among those living in mixed settlements of Butonese and non-Butonese, a group descended predominantly from nutmeg plantation labourers, and much less so among those associated with concentrated settlements of Butonese or enclaves that had developed on the periphery of the plantation system. It is among the latter populations that the Buton sultanate is far more likely to be mentioned as an important part of being Butonese.

Chauvel (1990:3) suggests that large-scale movement from the Buton region to Ambon, the nearby capital of Maluku, began in the late 19th century, the bulk of which was from Binongko.[6] However, the mixed communities of *orang Butung* and non-Butonese, closely associated with the locations of colonial-era nutmeg estates, are said to have existed for unrecalled generations. Certainly an early-17th-century observer mentions 'Bouttons' as among the wide array of peoples, both free and slaves, in the Bandas at that time (van de Wall 1934:552). Valentijn (1858:10), for example, who was resident in the islands in the latter 17th century, records a nutmeg estate named 'Boeton'. In 1795 Butonese are mentioned among free immigrants to the islands (Miller 1980:44). The Butonese enclaves in the Bandas, by contrast, trace their founding to the first decades of the 20th century. The largest of the enclaves had been located on the island of Gunung Api, an active volcano which was not used for nutmeg-growing. An eruption in 1988 caused the population of the island to be evacuated, the majority forming the settlement of Tanahrata on Neira Island and a smaller proportion moving to the hamlets of Waling Besar and Waling Kecil on Banda Besar Island.

These relocations served to underscore the differences in language use and naming style between the two segments of Banda's *orang Butung* population. A significant difference also involved discourse concerning the status of ancestors. Among the descendants of estate labourers, narratives of migration frequently stress their ancestors' low status as explaining the decision to depart from the Buton region. They suggest that *orang Butung* arriving in the Bandas throughout the colonial period were deliberately fleeing a system of corveé labour (*'kerja paksa'*, literally 'forced labour'). This was described as endemic to the Buton region, linked to the authority of the sultan and to a rigid hierarchical social order associated with the sultanate, which was fixed at birth and manifest in Butonese naming prefixes. In addition to *La* or *Wa*, higher-status individuals—a Butonese noble class—were identified locally as bearing the additional title Odé (eg La Odé Kulé). This was described as equivalent to the *raden* title in Java, or the Bugis term *andi*. At the time of the departure of their ancestors, the authority of the sultanate's nobility and the obligations of labour were described as harsh (*'kuasa dan kerja keras waktu itu'*).

If an Odé passed by a lower-ranking individual, the latter was said to have been obligated to make a gesture of obeisance, lifting the hands, palms pressed together, while lowering the head, a gesture known as *somba* in the Bandas (*'musti somba, angkat tangan'*). Marriage between Odé and non-Odé was forbidden; sexual interaction, if it occurred, would be severely punished. Other widespread claims suggested that Odé alone were allowed to wear shoes and to carry umbrellas as a sign of their rank. They were also permitted to wear the distinctive Malay brimless oval cap (*songko*) on a particular angle. If a lower-ranking person was seen wearing their *songko* on a similar angle by a passing Odé, they would be struck and the *songko* thrown to the ground. One informant's comments are typical: 'these are the stories the old people told... in the past, being Butonese in Buton [could involve] extreme hardship...they ill-treated [lower status people], that Odé class' (*'ini cerita-cerita yang orang tua-tua bilang...dulu itu paling keras, suku Butung kalau di Butung...dorang siksa, Odé-Odé dorang'*).

The *songko* narrative is especially compelling in the context of contemporary Bandanese life, where the cap is strongly associated with Muslim identity (Christians do not wear it) and Islamic practice (it is worn on all occasions involving prayer). To strike someone's *songko* into the dirt would constitute a shocking insult not just to the individual but to the spirit of Muslim community. Stories circulated about Muslim life in contemporary *kabupaten* Buton suggest that the circular seating layout associated with house-based prayer (*kerja rumah*) is arranged strictly according to hereditary rank. As a result, many orang Butung informants expressed trepidation at the thought of ever visiting the region because of their lack of knowledge concerning such matters; they might sit in the wrong place inadvertently, causing offence.[7] The narrative also served as a regular point of favourable comparison with the benefits of life in the Banda Islands, where men always urged others to move to the most respected positions in prayer gatherings, demurring when they are themselves urged to do the same. As one informant stated: 'over there [ie Buton] are fixed ranks. Outside [that region] they disappear, they are not relevant. Who am I? Who are you? It doesn't matter' (*'Di sana punya pangkat tetap saja. Di luar su tarada, tida apa. Beta siapa? Pané siapa? Tida apa'*). The Banda Islands are seen as far more socially egalitarian than Buton, a trait which is valorised in terms of the ideals of brotherhood within the Muslim 'community of believers' or *ummat*.

Those opposing the rigidly stratified social order of Buton were viewed as having a single option—to leave the islands. They are thought to have been predominantly men, who masked their intentions by ostensibly departing to fish or trade. In fact, they never returned. In some accounts, this is considered to have involved leaving behind wives, children and established households. Such a choice was often described in terms of reluctance and difficulty, but as ultimately necessary because of a lack of alternatives; open opposition to the social order was thought to have been punishable by imprisonment or even death. These departures were usually expressed in terms of *merantau*—to journey away from one's home area and settle elsewhere.

Merantau

In the view of many mixed-settlement Butonese, then, their ancestors' departure was forced by circumstances well beyond their control. In discussing issues of population displacement and mobility it is tempting to reach for the recently prominent but analytically ambiguous term 'diaspora'. Andaya (1995:119), for example, writes in historical terms of 'Bugis–Makassar diasporas', and Cummings (1998:107) mentions a 'Melaka Malay diaspora'. While it might seem possible to refer similarly to a Tukang Besi diaspora, or even to conceive of Butonese identification outside Buton in terms of 'diasporic community' (Clifford 1997:261), questions remain as to how useful such an expression is in capturing the multiple specificities of population movement and resettlement, and how appropriate its application across diverse socio-cultural contexts. In particular, treatments of diaspora frequently highlight discourses of home and return among the diasporic group, a continuing nostalgia concerning the homeland, and often also a feeling of provisionality or ambivalence at the host location.

In the Indonesia–Malay region, the existing discourse of *merantau* needs to be addressed as an integral part of any theoretical engagement with notions of diaspora. Wherever it occurs, *merantau* seems to mean leaving one's home, one's relatives, one's home village or country either temporarily, for a very long time or forever (Wang 1985:44). The concept of *merantau* suggests this may be necessary, beneficial, and even profitable; but it also need not involve any compulsion to return. Both *merantau* and diaspora, then, are able to refer to migration and to population mobility. However, in relation to the issue of displacement, there is some suggestion that *merantau* is not able to embrace all historically relevant causes of human mobility between locations, for example as the result of slavery or the fleeing of refugees (Wang 1985:44). Indeed, Andaya's (1995) use of 'diaspora' is in relation to refugees from local conflicts, just as Cummings (1998) applies the term to dislocations resulting from the fall of Melaka to the Portuguese in the 16th century.

In the context of recent large-scale, inter-communal conflicts in Sulawesi and Maluku, the term *pengungsi* or 'refugee' has attained a new prominence, describing a category of person subject to government scrutiny and management, often with the assistance of international agencies.[8] Several thousand Muslims sought refuge in the Banda Islands from conflicts in Maluku after January 1999. My impression in the Banda context is that *pengungsi* were very unlikely to be viewed as engaging in *merantau*. The emphasis appeared to be on their vulnerability and transitory state. The life of refugees is depicted as peculiarly dis-placed and vulnerable, but also one that is postponed rather than permanent. Research attention certainly needs to be given to the evolving social meanings of the category *pengungsi* in Indonesia and its relationship to other terms for population movements like *merantau*. The expression 'refugee', of course, has wide application in the West. One may now encounter economic refugees as well as political refugees, qualifications that encode complex moral and administrative judgements bearing acute practical consequences. By the same token, *merantau* can include, as Wang (1985:44) suggests, a wide range of the subtle aspects of willingness to move, deciding when and where to move to, even the range of possible reasons as to why an individual or group may want to migrate. In these specific senses, I would argue that *merantau* is as capable of embracing the conditions of displacement as the term diaspora.

More importantly, *merantau* has none of the cultural baggage often carried by the expression diaspora, lacking associations of ambivalence and nostalgia. Even where such elements are muted, diaspora has as its clear emphasis the state of dispersal itself far more than the conditions of departure. As a result, to be positioned as a member of a diaspora is to be, in a sense, perpetually displaced or liminal—defined by this state and to an extent by the past, far more than by emplacement and the present. By contrast, the capacity for agency that inheres to *merantau* creates much more space for the possibility of profound (re)connection with new locations. In addition, *merantau* is able to take fuller account of the many permutations of remembrance which can act to bring displacement to an end as much as foster a continuing urge to return 'home' (Fox 2001:67–8). Diaspora seems to hark back to territorialised visions of ethnicity even as it is used analytically to challenge such conceptions, evoking images of de-territorialised identities seen as a defining feature of globalisation (cf. Geschiere and Meyer 1998). *Merantau* seems entirely free of encodings of group membership: there is no generative shattering of ethnic homogeneity intrinsic to the discourse of *merantau*. There is instead departure (disconnection/displacement), movement and the possibility of re-settlement (re-connection/re-emplacement).

The Butonese of the enclave settlements differ from the Butonese of the mixed settlements in several respects when envisioning their in-migrating ancestors. The names of in-migrating community founders can often still be recalled, and it is notable that these inevitably include a number of Odé (ie high-status) figures. There is also a noticeable absence of talk about fleeing forced labour or social hardship. The emphasis in accounting for departure is on environmental explanations—the poor or stony soils of Wakatobi, and the lack of viable farming land there or on Buton and Muna Islands. Their ancestors are also described as leaving Tukang Besi in order to *merantau*, but the stress on this term in the enclave settlements involves an active quest for good fortune, or in local terminology *cari rijiki* (literally [to] seek good luck). This latter expression is imbued with meaning—at once meeting one's fate, but also involving the potential exercise of individual spiritual power, of testing one's mettle, and of gaining magical knowledge (*ilmu*) from powerful sources.

After their arrival in the Banda Islands, these ancestors are represented as creating an existence through resourcefulness, usually involving trading and fishing. The name of one Butonese settlement, Panti Sero (on Neira Island), celebrates a form of tidal-fence fish-trap (*sero*) that was used at the location by colonial-era Butonese in-migrants. Gunung Api residents were still described as the most knowledgeable in weaving the bamboo submersible fish-traps known as *bubu*. Such activities were frequently contrasted in historical terms with the option of joining the nutmeg estates as labourers. Indeed, the (non-Butonese) estate labourers of the colonial period were often spoken of in the enclave communities in disparaging terms such as 'contract people' (*orang kontrak*, ie indentured) or, more pejoratively, even as 'coolies' (*kuli*) and 'ragged paupers' (*orang buruk*). This latter term in particular carries definite connotations of being somewhat shiftless, and certainly not an agent of spiritual potency, attracting good fortune through the exercise of *ilmu*.

(Re)emplacement

Carsten (1997:272) suggests that low-status groups, those at the bottom of hierarchical orders and the impoverished, are always among the most mobile of any population.[9] Among such groups there is often little reason to recall past genealogical details, and indeed in the Bandas this knowledge is shallow—generally two or three generations at most, and interest in such matters is limited. What might be termed a 'future orientation' to kinship knowledge is emphasised, a feature common among societies in which mobility is a central feature of social life. In such contexts, 'it may be more important to create kinship out of new ties than to remember ancestors whose identity has become largely irrelevant' (Carsten 1997:273).

Under these circumstances a sense of connectedness to place and to people is not sought or derived from past ties but must be created in the future. In a related sense, the existence of cognatic modes of reckoning kin (ie tracing relatedness through both the mother and the father) has been linked by anthropologists to small island environments, where the consequent ability to maximise the extension of kin-relations creates a potential resource for the continuing out-migration (*merantau*) of younger generations. This 'wide' rather than 'deep' tracking of relatedness again makes particular sense when situated in a regional context where maritime trade and the movement of people have been pivotal features over thousands of years. In the Bandas, the Butonese population generally shares this future orientation to kinship with non-Butonese. The latter also do not reckon genealogy more than two or three generations prior to the present, can rarely name more than the general region that in-migrating ancestors originated from, and also stress the essential commonality of these ancestors' contract-labour status.

In addition to escaping systems of rank, mixed-settlement Butonese informants often spoke of their ancestors as having discarded other traditions (*adat*) associated with Buton or as leaving them behind ('*su buang adat itu, su kasih tinggal saja*'). People suggested that if one's ancestors carry *adat* practice from one place to another their children and grandchildren will tend to feel obligated to continue it, perhaps even afraid to risk the consequences of not doing so (eg attracting illness or other misfortune). Their out-migrating Butonese ancestors are depicted as having been wise in deciding that *adat Butung* would be too burdensome for their descendants in the new location and therefore took the opportunity of intentionally leaving it behind (and bearing any consequences themselves). Their descendants often expressed gratitude, viewing *adat Butung* as expensive and also as involving too many ritual restrictions (*kerja pomali*) concerning men and women, none of which they observe.

An associated perspective is that *adat* belongs primarily to place–earth, and to an emplaced community, not to people (*'tanah punya bukan orang punya'*). In this understanding, *adat Butung* could be left behind because it was no longer relevant to in-migrants who had to adapt themselves (*sesuai diri*) to their new location. This explanation was sometimes offered as the reason for the persistence of *adat Butung* among the enclave communities, especially on Gunung Api. This island lacks the traditional polities (*negeri adat*) found elsewhere in the Bandas and therefore has no *adat* of place which demands recognition (cf. Winn 1998; 2001). Butonese in the mixed communities are welcome to participate in the local ritual events associated with the *negeri adat* where they reside and many have taken this option, even gaining prominence through occupying important ritual positions. Agency is always stressed alongside local birth as a critical factor in making the shift from primary identification as *orang Butung* to *orang Banda*. This may never entirely eradicate their Butonese identity from the perspective of non-Butonese, and indeed some Butonese themselves consider the possibility of enduring descent-based affiliation to *bangsa suku* (ethnic group), the authorised forms of cultural diversity disseminated by the Indonesian state. However, it can meaningfully overlay and even displace it: 'I have Banda origins because I was born in Banda' (*'beta berasal di Banda karna lahir di Banda'*). As with much of Banda's contemporary population, outsider origins does not exclude the possibility of expressing claims to a legitimate and thoroughly emplaced (though non-autochthonous) local identity.

Among the enclave Butonese, there was no comparable discourse of 'throwing away' *adat Butung*. Since the eruption of Gunung Api, the settlements have been located within the areas of the traditional polities of Banda, but few if any of the residents are active participants in local ritual events, despite regular invitations to attend, preferring to be spectators only. Nonetheless, even in the main *Butung* concentrations of the Bandas, considerable intermarriage between Odé and non-Odé has been occurring for some time—an act they agree would be impossible under the historical strictures of rank in the Tukang Besi Islands themselves, and one that reputedly remains difficult, and certainly expensive, in the Buton area.[10] It was not unusual to hear the Odé title itself (particularly among the non-Odé) described as somewhat archaic. Many adults have begun to discard this component of their naming affixes, expressing discomfort with the overt assertion of differential status it conveys, referring to the term as a sign of a 'bureaucratic' and even 'feudal' system. Butonese *adat* within the enclave communities tended to be viewed as neither irrelevant nor prohibitively costly, but rather as a body of practice from which negative elements might be discarded and the positive retained.

The guide to such choices was usually described as being Islam. In common with the mixed-settlement Butonese (and perhaps as a result of their influence) the loss of the Odé naming component was being seen as more compatible with ideals of Muslim *ummat* and also as resting more easily alongside ideas of shared citizenship. The La and Wa prefixes were less disposable in their function of overtly referring to and affirming Muslim identity. Also unlike Butonese in the mixed settlements, the loss of language was a source of some concern. Numerous informants expressed profound embarrassment at the lack of skills in *bahasa Butung* among their children, and disquiet at the implication this might carry for their ability to claim Butonese identity, especially with other Butonese outside the Banda Islands. As a result, teachers at schools in the enclave settlements had commenced Butonese language and culture classes. The latter tended to emphasise learning a Butonese folk-dance (*tarian Butung*) to be performed at civic occasions, especially Indonesian Independence Day (*Hari Kemerdekaan*). The dance was drawn from a more involved coming-of-age/menarche ceremony for young women, known as *pajogé*, rarely practised any longer by Banda Butonese throughout the islands. Informants stated that young women had become unwilling to take part and their parents were reluctant to force the issue, just as school-age children were disinclined to use even the basic forms of the Butonese naming prefix. Many older informants observed somewhat resignedly that young people here, as everywhere, preferred to 'follow the crowd' ('*ikut ramai*')—in this case, the majority non-Butonese Bandanese.

Conclusion

There is clearly a range of factors bearing on the differences I have discussed between the two segments of the Butonese population in the Banda Islands. Longer, multi-generational residence and higher rates of marriage with non-Butonese are both features of the mixed settlements not raised here in any detail, and highly relevant to issues of language use. The religious affiliation of the Butonese as Muslims, the status of this religion as predominant among the non-Buton population of the Bandas, and the latter's representation of place-oriented ritual practice as both autochthonous and Islamic all contribute to the relative permeability of contemporary Bandanese identity in the islands.

Nevertheless, the marked differences between the two Butonese segments in depictions of migrant ancestors and in Butonese *adat* practice suggest that specific conditions of departure can play a significant role in the relative dynamics of emplacement within a mobile population, in addition to shaping views of the homeland left behind. Perhaps as importantly, the example of the Butonese in the Bandas illustrates the variability within even relatively small and co-located *émigré* populations. In writing about representations of Chinese diaspora, Ang (1993:19) argues that:

> what it means to be Chinese varies from place to place, moulded by local circumstances in which peoples of Chinese ancestry have settled and constructed new ways of living. There are, in other words, many different Chinese identities, not one.

This is likely to be true also of the Butonese communities scattered throughout eastern Indonesia. We need to be careful that terms such as diaspora and ethnicity are used in ways that avoid foreclosing the possibilities of difference, and to recognise the strategic uses of essentialism within expressions of collective identity. Where an alternative and localised discourse exists that is able to address simultaneously departure, displacement and (re)emplacement— such as *merantau*—it ought to be considered a potentially useful means of escaping the limitations of our own intervening assumptions.

Endnotes

1   In the earliest historical sense, the term 'Moluccas' generally referred to the northern clove-growing islands in what is now the province of North Maluku, especially the sultanates of Ternate and Tidore. The Banda Islands lay outside this area, but were nevertheless a key location in the area's spice trade. Many spice merchants never visited the northern sultanates, but relied on Banda's burgeoning entrepôt role importing cloves from the north to trade alongside its own nutmeg and mace.

2   This holds not as a simple numerical total, but in the sense of possessing the highest proportion of ships to population. Southon (1995:47) provides figures from 1987 giving Binongko a people-to-trading-boat (*perahu lambo*) ratio of 63:1 (population 11,152 and 175 *lambo*). Wanci, despite its 222 trading vessels, had a population of 32,069, giving a ratio of 144:1 (Tomia 93:1; Kaledupa 278:1).

3   Speakers of more than one variety often observed that *bahasa Biningko* and *bahasa Tomia* are much the same, with *bahasa Wanci* more distinctive. In linguistic terms, the populations of the Tukang Besi Islands are viewed as speaking related languages, long considered four dialects of a single language (Noorduyn 1991:131). Donohue (1995:8) describes dialect differences more systematically and suggests that it may be appropriate to regard northern (Wanci and Kaledupa) and southern (Binongko and Tomia) Butonese as two distinct, though very closely related languages. Within these two broad divisions, each island has its own distinct speech, distinguished both lexically and allophonically, in addition to several sub-dialects (Donohue 1995:8).

4   Direct quotes appearing in italics represent examples of mother-tongue Malay use in the Banda Islands, which often varies from the standardised Malay adopted as the national language of Indonesia (*Bahasa Indonesia*). It may represent an identifiable dialect; certainly, historical accounts refer to the existence of a distinctively local 'Banda Malay' spoken in the islands, contrasting for example with the Ambonese Malay that has come to form an important *lingua franca* in central and southeast Maluku (see for example Grimes 1991).

5   Informants linked the affix *La* to the first section of the Muslim affirmation of belief '*La ilahha ilalah*' ('there is no God but Allah') and *Wa* to the phrase '*Wa Rahmatullahi wa barakatu*' ('and the mercy of God and His blessings') appearing commonly in prayer and the introduction to a formal address of any kind.

6   As noted earlier, this expression may well have formed a synonym for the Tukang Besi Islands as a whole.

7   The capital of both sultanate and *kabupaten* Buton is at Bau-Bau, a port town on Buton Island that is directly connected to the Banda Islands (via Ambon) by a regular route of inter-island passenger ships.

8   For a general discussion of recent communal violence in eastern Indonesia see Pannell (2003); with reference to the Banda Islands in particular, see Winn (2003).

9   A point overlooked in the current climate, where globalisation is embraced as the unhindered flow of capital, but the movement of people—particularly the poor—is

restricted or rejected. This contradictory response is as economically ill-informed (imagining that capital and labour are somehow unrelated) as it is unsustainable socially.

10 Informants suggest that larger than usual marriage prestations from the family of a non-Odé individual can be used to smooth the process with an Odé individual's family.

Bugis migration to Samarinda, East Kalimantan: establishing a colony?

Riwanto Tirtosudarmo

Introduction

Since 1996 Indonesia has been rocked by a series of violent conflicts. The first large violent conflict broke out in December 1996 in Sanggau-Ledo sub-district in Sambas, West Kalimantan, between Madurese migrants and local Dayaks. Social, religious and ethnic conflict has become a seemingly permanent feature of the post-Soeharto political landscape. In the series of communal conflicts, the migrant population has always been involved. In many cases, entire migrant communities have been transformed into victims forced to leave their settlement areas, such as the Madurese in West and Central Kalimantan and the Butonese in Ambon, Maluku. The involvement of migrants in conflict with local populations of differing ethnic backgrounds raises the serious question of the relationship between migration and ethnic conflict. A 2002 study on the anatomy of violence in Indonesia in the preceeding years found that communal and separatist violence caused the greatest amount of fatalities, accounting for 77% and 22% respectively. While social violence was not uncommon during the Soeharto regime, social violence and fatalities increased dramatically during the period of transition to democracy, reaching its peak in 1999/2000. The study also shows that in cases of communal violence, ethnic–religion–migration related violence alone contributed to around 52% of total deaths (see Tadjoeddin 2002).

This paper is about migration of the Bugis to Samarinda, the capital city of East Kalimantan province. The Bugis are the dominant ethnic group in South Sulawesi and, alongside the Minangkabaus of West Sumatra, the Madurese from Madura island and the Banjarese of South Kalimantan, one of Indonesia's major ethnic groups with a strong tradition of migration. The Bugis migrated with their ships and settled almost all areas of the archipelago, in several places constituting a dominant ethnic group. East Kalimantan is one of the prime destinations for Bugis settlement. East Kalimantan is also a destination for Banjarese from South Kalimantan, Torajans from Central Sulawesi, and Florenese from East Nusa Tenggara. The state-sponsored transmigration programs have also targeted East Kalimantan as a major destination since the 1970s.[1]

The relatively peaceful situation in East Kalimantan, in comparison with the explosive conditions found in West and Central Kalimantan, shows that migrant and local populations do not invariably conflict, although social tensions are always a natural part of the adjustment process between people from different ethnic backgrounds in East Kalimantan. The experience of the Bugis migrant community in Samarinda and East Kalimantan on the whole demonstrates that they have not only been successful in adjusting in a new place, but also have contributed significantly to establishing a new multi-ethnic society strongly dominated by Bugis culture. The Bugis settlement in East Kalimantan provides a strikingly different case from the experience of the Madurese in West and Central Kalimantan, who have been constantly in conflict with the local population. The domination of the Bugis in the fields of economy and politics has insulated East Kalimantan from these difficulties simply because the Bugis colony is acknowledged as dominant and well-established.

A brief historical background

According to Christian Pelras, a French anthropologist who has studied the Bugis for decades, Bugis settlements outside South Sulawesi have been established in the archipelago since the end of the 17th century. So by the end of the 18th century, Bugis settlements could be found in Sumatra, such as in Bengkulu and in the Riau islands, in the Malay peninsula, in Kalimantan, among other places in and around Pontianak, Mempawah, Pulau Laut, Pagatan, Pasir, Kutai, Samarinda, Bulungan and Gunung Tabur. In the east of the Makassar straits, the Bugis settled in Palu bay, in Donggala, Banawa and Kaili, in Sumbawa. In Java, the Bugis settled mostly in port cities, like Surabaya, Gresik and Batavia. After the 18th century, the Bugis also settled in Indragiri and Jambi in Sumatra, along the west coast of Johor and Sabah in East Malaysia and around Lake Lindu and the southeast of Sulawesi. In the 19th and 20th centuries, Bugis settlements were founded in eastern Indonesia, including Maluku, Papua and East Timor. Since the early 1980s, the three ethnic groups originally from South Sulawesi—the Bugis, the Butonese and the Makasarese—have gained notoriety in eastern Indonesia as the BBM. Tensions and conflicts with the local population have been common in Papua and East Timor since the early 1990s (Aditjondro 1986; Tirtosudarmo 1997).

The reasons for Bugis migration, as for other ethnic groups, are always complex. On this, Pelras (1996:320) said that stories told by and about Bugis tend to emphasise how Bugis migration is related to 'the resolution of personal conflict, an affront received, political insecurity or the desire to escape either unsatisfactory social conditions or undesirable repercussions of an act of violence perpetrated at home'. While such factors are insufficient to account for the ongoing nature of Bugis migration and other reasons including economic factors must also be adduced, it is interesting to note that Bugis do not relate migration solely to economic matters. Another characteristic that Pelras mentions with regard to Bugis migration is the structural pressures that make each period develop push as well pull factors for the Bugis migration from their place of origin in South Sulawesi. Another Bugis expert, Lineton (1975:9), argued that the Bugis:

> are peculiarly dependent upon their relationships with other regions for the maintenance of their society in its present form…As a result of political and economic pressures, the Bugis have, over a period of at least three centuries – become increasingly integrated within the wider socio-economic system of the Malay world.

Lineton (1975:22) noted four characteristics of the Bugis migrant settlements:

• the destination is usually a less densely populated area;

• the site is usually in swampy lowlands that have a heavy rainy season particularly suitable for growing rice, and that will one day turn into a coconut plantation. At first sight, the Bugis settlement looks like an unattractive swamp area, but in fact it represents a potentially very profitable ecological niche;

• they are close to a seaport accessible with their boats, giving them a convenient place to bring their agriculture produce to market;

• the potential for future settlement expansion to adjacent areas.

A study of Bugis migration from Wajo shows that the largest out migration flows occurred during the period of the Kahar Muzakkar rebellion between 1950 and 1965. The population of Wajo, particularly in the rural areas, faced a dilemma. According to the study of Kalola village, located around 23 kilometres north of the Wajo district seat Sengkang, the residents were caught between the rebels and the Indonesian military. This phenomenon shows the high level of insecurity and feelings of vulnerability experienced by the people of Kalola (see Bisri 1985). Out-migration had become their most rational alternative. The people of Kalola usually migrated to Jambi and Indragiri in Sumatra, Toli-Toli in Sulawesi, and Samarinda in East Kalimantan. To finance their migration, some sold their land to their neighbours who decided to stay in the village. They migrated in groups from the port of Makassar via Tanjung Priok harbour in Jakarta, then on to their destinations in Sumatra. The people who migrated to Samarinda and Toli-Toli boarded their boats in Pare-Pare. The massive movement left Kalola almost empty. It was reported, for instance, that in Lawartanae—the main village of Kalola—out of around 300 households, only 30 households remained. Langkautu, which had 100 households, and Awatanae, which had 200 households, were found during the study to be deserted (Bisri 1985:16–17).

Social disruption and political chaos were clearly strong push factors for massive Bugis migration from Kalola to the land beyond. South Sulawesi communities have long been characterised by insecurity. During colonial times, conflicts not only occurred between the Dutch and the *aru* or *karaeng* but also between the *aru* and the *karaeng* themselves (Ahimsa Putra 1988:143–144). The end of hostilities following the killing of Kahar Muzakkar on 3 February 1965 apparently did not stop Bugis migration from Kalola, though the volume decreased somewhat.[2] According to Bisri (1985:19), it was difficult for people in Kalola to stay, as the neglected land became increasingly difficult to plough. Another factor that pushed the remaining people in Kalola to migrate came with the news that their fellow villagers had succeeded in the new settlements. Rice harvest failures in 1971 and 1972 caused by the drought convinced further numbers of Kalola to move to the new settlements.

Migration and trade networks

Bugis migration to East Kalimantan increased markedly after the 1970s, as shown by the increased number of regular passenger ship journeys between Pare-Pare and Balikpapan and Samarinda. Among these ships are the large PELNI ships, such as the Tidar, Binaiya, and the smaller private ships, the Teratai, Tanjung Salamat and Samarinda Ekspres. Other large PELNI ships were available from Makassar to Balikpapan, the Kambuna and the Kerinci. Bugis migration patterns, particularly as concerns the traders, have changed, as can be seen from patterns of capital ownership. Migrants arriving in East Kalimantan around the 1970s generally obtained their capital from relatives and friends. In the 1980s the Bugis migrants in East Kalimantan, particularly Samarinda, known as *migran baru* (the new migrants), no longer relied on their families or close friends in acquiring the capital, but from any source whatsoever, not necessarily Bugis.

The so called 'old Bugis' in Samarinda mostly settled in the area known as 'Samarinda-Seberang', on the south side of the Mahakam River in the city of Samarinda. These people are believed to be the descendants of the first generation of Bugis migrants to East Kalimantan. Some of these people are traders originally from Wajo district in South Sulawesi who still maintain close cultural and economic relations with Bugis elsewhere. A business trader the author met on a passenger ship travelling from Makassar to Balikpapan explained that he dealt in numerous commodities. He supplied goods according to the seasons. Any commodity that is available either in South Sulawesi or East Kalimantan may be traded, depending on the demand of the market on both sides. This phenomenon supports Pelras' observation that adopting the market economy is strongly characteristic of the Bugis migration strategy. According to this Wajo trader, if the market in Samarinda wants coconuts, he will send coconuts from Pare-Pare to Samarinda. If the people in Wajo are harvesting peanuts, he will go back to East Kalimantan with a full load of them. He admitted that in both Wajo and Samarinda he already had a strong network consisting of fellow Bugis and Chinese traders.

For the Bugis traders, East Kalimantan is not just a destination within their trading network, but a second home beyond Wajo or South Sulawesi. In East Kalimantan, the Bugis traders also have long had a reputation as mediators and brokers for other traders in the border areas between Indonesia and East Malaysia. In Tarakan, a town close to the border, for example, the Bugis are well known as traders who bring various commodities, including electronic appliances and cloth, from the Tanah Abang market in Jakarta. From a cursory observation made by the author in Pare-Pare harbour, ships heading to Tarakan and Nunukan (the closest town to Sabah, East Malaysia) are loaded with rice coming from various places in South Sulawesi, particularly from the well-known rice-producing district of Wajo. It is said that rice from Wajo is exported to Sabah. Pare-Pare, beside its role as a trading harbour is also an important embarkation port for migrant workers en route to work in East Malaysia, particularly Sabah. The labour migrants mostly come from South Sulawesi and East Nusa Tenggara, particularly the Florenese from East Flores district.

A study conducted by Parta (1996) in the central Citra-Niaga market in downtown Samarinda, shows that there is no particular ethnic dominance among shop owners. Ethnicity is a differentiating factor in the kinds of commodities sold in the shops. For instance, Banjarese sell jewellery and souvenirs, Javanese sell cooked foods in their *warungs* (small restaurants), Bugis usually sell cloth, shoes, electrical appliances and fruit. The Dayak traders sell ethnic souvenirs, often identifying themselves as Kutais. In the mid-1980s, an observer admitted the difficulties involved in estimating the population of Samarinda according to ethnicity:

> From my casual observations in the city and from reading 1980 provincial level census data I argue that the last decade has seen a rapid increase in the number of migrants from other islands in the Indonesian archipelago. An important trend is the growing percentage of Javanese, particularly from East Java, moving into the city. An older but still significant migrant stream of Buginese from South Sulawesi is also helping to shape the ethnic composition of the city (Wood 1985:131–132).

While a reliable source on the ethnic background of the dominant group in East Kalimantan is lacking, partial studies, among others by Magenda (1989), show that the Bugis are dominant, along with the Javanese, in the local bureaucracy in East Kalimantan, especially in the provincial government. The Bugis are also believed to be the dominant group in economic sectors, particularly in trade and transportation. According to Peluso (1987), in East Kalimantan the Bugis always assume a crucial role when conflict or war occurs between ethnic groups. For example, in colonial times, the Bugis played an important role in defending the Kutais from attack by the hinterland Dayak. The Bugis also defended the Kutai sultanate from the invasion of the Dutch as well as the Sulus who came from Mindanao in the Philippines.

The Bugis community in Samarinda Seberang: a home away from home

Samarinda-Seberang is believed by the people in Samarinda to be the oldest Bugis settlement in Samarinda and perhaps in East Kalimantan. As noted by Pelras (1996:321–322), the Bugis have been in Samarinda since at least the early 18th century,

In the early eighteenth century the Wajo' prince La Ma'dukelleng, Arung of Singkang [Sengkang] and a fierce opponent of the Dutch and their Boné allies, left South Sulawesi with a group of about 3,000 followers for Pasir in east Borneo, just across the Makassar strait from South Sulawesi, where a small community of Bugis traders from Wajo' was already established. Engaging in trade, he stayed there until 1737, when he returned to South Sulawesi as the newly elected Arung Matoa of Wajo' to wage war against Boné and its Dutch allies...In east Borneo, La Ma'dukelleng concluded political matrimonial alliances with local rulers just as he would have done in his home country; thus he married one of his sons to one of the Sultan of Pasir's daughters and, later, their daughter to Sultan Idris of Kutei [Kutai], while he himself became Sultan of Pasir. He was also active in organizing further Wajo' communities all down the east coast of Borneo, each under its elected chiefs.

Having obtained from the previous Sultan of Kutei the right of settlement for Bugis in Samarinda, a strategic settlement near the mouth of the Mahakam river, somewhat downriver from the Kutei capital, he later also obtained from Sultan Idris monopoly rights over the export of products from the hinterland, including gold-dust, benzoin, camphor, damar, gaharu wood, rattan, bird's-nests, beeswax, bezoar stones and rhinoceros horn (for which, however, only Kutei Malays were permitted to trade upriver), and of sea products such as tortoiseshell, turtles' eggs, agar-agar and trepang. The Samarinda Bugis also had the monopoly on imports of rice, salt, spices, coffee, tobacco, opium, chinaware, textiles, iron, firearms, saltpetre and slaves. Moreover, their right to self-government was recognized and they organized themselves under the authority of a chief entitled Pua' Ado (the daughter of the first bearer of this title had married another of La Ma'dukelleng's sons) and a council of a number of *nakhoda* or rich sea traders. Some Bugis leaders were granted titles by the Sultan which put them on a par with the Malay nobility and qualified them for intermarriage with the ruling dynasty. The Samarinda Bugis eventually obtained the right to control the upriver trade, and a Bugis was appointed *shahbandar*, an officer whose main function was to levy port taxes.

Pelras, in his book *The Bugis*, shows that the pattern and the process of migration that eventually formed a Bugis settlement differs from one settlement to another. The migration process of the Bugis in Samarinda, as shown above, indicates that political and economic changes both in South Sulawesi and in the land beyond play an important role in determining the existence and development of Bugis settlements. Economy certainly plays an important role, and migration also can be seen as a Bugis market-economy strategy. This is supported by Acciaioli (1998) who studied in the surrounding areas of Lake Lindu in Central Sulawesi how effectively the Bugis adjust their economic strategy to the market and price fluctuation of the agricultural products for export.

Samarinda-Seberang is an old Bugis settlement located almost in the centre of Samarinda, the provincial capital of East Kalimantan. This area comprises two *desa*, Baka and Masjid. This Bugis community in Samarinda-Seberang is particularly well known for its *sarung* weaving industry which, interestingly, is known as *sarung* Samarinda (not *sarung* Bugis). It is a home industry employing mostly women. In small sample survey of 145 households, conducted in July–August 1999, fewer than half of the persons surveyed were born in South Sulawesi (most of them hailing from Wajo district). The other half were mostly born in Samarinda—as the second or third generation since migration.

This proves that Bugis settlement in the area is long established. The large proportion of the Bugis born in Samarinda-Seberang also indicates that migration seems no longer to be an important phenomenon for the Bugis in Samarinda-Seberang. The survey reveals that the migrants, who migrated from South Sulawesi, ranged in age from one to 30 years. Perhaps permanent migration will decline, and circulation will become the new pattern of Bugis migration, from South Sulawesi to Samarinda-Seberang. The improvement of sea transportation from South Sulawesi definitely plays a significant role in changing the pattern of Bugis migration to Samarinda-Seberang from permanent to circular.

In Samarinda-Seberang, where Bugis culture dominates, another change is demonstrated by the findings of the survey. Among the women workers in the *sarung* industry, 103 were born in Samarinda, while only 76 were born in Wajo and 19 were from other places in South Sulawesi. It shows that the ability and the skill to weave *sarung* had already been transferred to Samarinda. Weaving as part of the Bugis culture is a form of social cultural capital that is no longer the monopoly of Wajo but has been preserved and developed by Bugis migrants, and passed on to the younger generation in Samarinda. If the *sarung* industry in Samarinda demands more labour, as often happens in a given period, employers will hasten to recruit in South Sulawesi for temporay employment in Samarinda-Seberang.

During the author's visit to Sabbangparu, a sub-district in Wajo that is well known for its *sarung* production, in August 1999, there were only three houses still involved in the *sarung* business. Each house only operated one loom. In interviews, the grim fact was revealed that the monetary crisis had devastated the industry. The price of imported thread for *sarung* had drastically increased to a point beyond the means of the owners of the *sarung* industry.[3] In order to survive, the people in Wajo turned to agriculture, planting cocoa, particularly for export. Everywhere, people were planting cocoa, and as a result the *sarung* industry was practically extinguished in Wajo. You have to go to Samarinda-Seberang in East Kalimantan now to find the Bugis expertise in weaving *sarung*. Another factor that has also contributed to the decline of the *sarung* Bugis home industry is the rapid expansion of large *sarung* factories in Java, in Gresik (East Java), Pekalongan (Central Java) and Majalaya (West Java), since the government invited foreign investment in the textile industry.

The ease of movement between the ports of Pare-Pare and Samarinda makes both places a continuum of sorts. In this continuum, massive movements of people occur in shorter and shorter time periods. It could be argued that this demographic phenomenon of population mobility has removed administrative and geographic boundaries between provinces.[4] As an indication, a man who runs a *sarung* Samarinda business and now lives in Samarinda-Seberang describes how convenient it is to move by saying he could be 'leaving Samarinda in the morning and by tomorrow afternoon have arrived in Pare-Pare'. Population mobility in this context has become the bridge linking two areas that are geographically separated; but then, as time goes by, culture is also flowing and slowly becoming integrated into a larger Bugis cultural domain.

Ethnic relations and the potential for conflict

As a province that attracts many migrants, East Kalimantan has long been of interest to scholars, particularly those studying the relationship between ethnic groups. Peluso (1987), for example, focuses on the relationship between the Kutais, the Dayaks and the Bugis in connection with the trade economy before the arrival of the Dutch, noting Lineton's view that in the 17th century the Bugis had already been given a strategic role by the Sultan of Kutai to defend the sultanate from attack by the Dayak who live in the hinterlands. Peluso states:

> The Sultan's troubles with the Dayaks may have motivated him to grant the Bugis settlement rights in the territory now called Samarinda, the site of his capital at the time, as well as giving them a trade monopoly on the product of the interior. Furthermore Lineton argued, in exchange for these 'rights' of settlement, Bugis trader-warriors were to protect the sultan from 'hostile outsiders', including headhunting groups living beyond the bounds of the sultanate and Tausug or rival Bugis groups from other kingdoms. To this end, the Bugis supplied the sultan with warriors for his army as well as the firearms to equip those armies (Peluso 1987:11).

Since Indonesian independence, studies on ethnic relationships in East Kalimantan have been conducted in connection with the transmigration program. A study by Fulcher (1983) shows that acculturation is not happening between the Javanese transmigrants and the local Dayak. Evers, Clauss & Gerke (1988) also indicated that trading networks are not developing between the Javanese and the Kutais as each group still primarily lives within their own trading networks. A study on local politics by Magenda (1989) shows that the Bugis have successfully penetrated the local bureaucracy.

In East Kalimantan, the Dayaks and the Kutais are known as the indigenous populations while the Javanese, the Bugis and the Banjarese are regarded as migrants. According to an informant (a Dayak intellectual at the University of Mulawarman), before the 1970s, the population of the Dayak and the Malay was 40 to 60, but now has become 50 to 50. He believes that the ethnic compositional change has resulted from a strengthening of Dayak identity, because some of the Dayak who previously preferred to be called Malay are now reasserting themselves as Dayak.[5] The revitalisation of Dayak identity, according to him, has occured because Dayakness has become a unifying identity marker in relation with others, namely the Malay, the Banjar, the Bugis or the Madurese. Religion also plays an important role in the relationship between ethnic groups in East Kalimantan. He further explained that the strengthening of Dayak identity is also instigated by the perception among the Dayaks that they constitute an underdeveloped and oppressed group. The depletion of natural resources, especially deforestation, significantly contributes to increasing tension between the locals and the migrants, as the declining economic resources result in growing competition between ethnic groups, especially between the locals and the migrants.

After the ethnic conflict in West Kalimantan between the locals and the Madurese migrants in 1997, a need was felt in East Kalimantan to build forums or an association of different ethnic groups in order to monitor and control the possibility of ethnic conflict. On 26 January 1999, the elders of each ethnic group in East Kalimantan came together to establish a Forum Komunikasi Persaudaraan Antar Masyarakat Kalimantan Timur [Forum of Communication and Brotherhood for the People of East Kalimantan].[6]

For the Dayak of East Kalimantan, the violent ethnic conflicts in West Kalimantan, and later in Central Kalimantan, between the locals (particularly the Dayak) and the Madurese migrants have further strengthened their perception of being indigenous. This, for example, prompted the establishment of Dayak organisation Ikatan Keluarga Pedalaman [Brotherhood of Hinterland People] particularly among the educated Dayak. The Dayak network has linked Dayak members not only in Kalimantan (Indonesia) but also in Sarawak and Sabah. This observation, for instance, is supported by an emerging issue in several Dayak districts near the border with East Malaysia, and is strongly related to the local response to the regional autonomy laws introduced in the post-Soeharto era[7]. As has occurred in other provinces in Indonesia, the demand to form a new province is also growing in East Kalimantan. Following the establishment of new regencies (Nunukan and Malinau) and the new Kotamadya (Tarakan), a discourse on the need to develop a new province in the north of East Kalimantan began to circulate, having first been proposed by the *bupati* of Berau, Bulungan and Tarakan. These three local leaders argued that the new province was needed to accelerate development in the north, particularly in the border areas that have traditionally been neglected by both provincial and central government.

While ethnicity and indigeneity have never been used in the discourse, casual observers will easily recognise that these elements are among the main factors behind the movement; this in fact is the political demand among the people in the North—to be recognised as the owner of the region and its resources. The movement should therefore be seen as part of the emergence of identity politics in Indonesia—a new political development that is moving in parallel with the confusing implementation of the decentralisation and regional autonomy laws. In East Kalimantan, this movement is still growing but apparently not as quickly as expected.

Conclusion

The Bugis, in Samarinda and East Kalimantan generally, have long established their settlements, and more importantly have developed a strong

Bugis cultural domain in the land beyond South Sulawesi. While in number, as reported by the population census in 2000, they are the second largest population after the Javanese, their long established settlements have provided a strong basis for their significant penetration of local economy and politics. Resentment towards the migrants in East Kalimantan has emerged, particularly among the local Dayak, who feel marginalised by the economic and political domination of the non-Dayak populations. Yet, as we have seen, this resentment has not erupted into the violence conflicts we have witnessed in West and Central Kalimantan. While a proper investigation should be conducted to explain the reasons for this, my observations suggest two factors that might be behind these phenomena.

The first is the difficulty for the Dayak to mobilise their resentment into a wider movement, as their number is proportionally small compared with the migrants, and their settlements are concentrated in the hinterland districts, mostly in the northern part of the province. The second factor is related to the fact that, aside from their large number, migrants, especially the Bugis, the Banjar and the Javanese, have deeply penetrated the local economy and political structure, and it would now be difficult for the locals to campaign against these groups in East Kalimantan.

The regional autonomy laws, however, provide a new political arena that can be used for mobilising the politics of belonging, in which ethnicity and territoriality may be manipulated to become a political vehicle for opposing domination by those considered outsiders.[8] The movement by local elites in the northern districts of East Kalimantan to demand a separate province—the proposed North Kalimantan or Kaltara province (propinsi Kalimantan Utara)— can be seen as the manifestation of this new politics, the politics of identity based on ethnicity.

Endnotes

1   Kutai district has become the main destination for transmigrants to East Kalimantan, receiving almost 50% of the provincial total. The official statistics from the Department of Transmigration show the number of transmigrants resettled during the New Order period as follows: Pelita I (1969–1973) 1,775 families, Pelita II (1974–1978) 3,311 families, Pelita III (1979–1983) 11,878 families, Pelita IV (1984–1988) 15,179 families, Pelita V (1989–1993) 16,525 families, and Pelita VI (1994–1997) 14,054 families (Tirtosudarmo 1998).

2   Lineton (1975:23) provides an interesting comment on Kahar Muzakkar's rebellion against the central government: 'the most important aim of the rebellion has in fact

been achieved: all the offices of government, from the lowest level of administration up to the provincial governor, are now filled by local-born people'.

3   In the statistical book *Kabupaten Wajo Dalam Angka 1998*, published by the District Level Bureau of Statistics, there is not a single sarung weaver remaining in the Wajo district.

4   Lineton (1975:1) also observes a similar phenomenon: 'the sending and the receiving areas are seen to be parts of a single society, each of which influences and is in turn affected by the other'. In the case of Bugis migration to Jambi, for instance, Lineton describes a place that:

> provides opportunities for economic and political advancement which are absent or limited in the Bugis homeland...It is possible indeed that migration is necessary for the continued functioning of many of the institutions of Bugis society, in particular the system of social stratification and political domination by an aristocratic elite (Lineton 1975:3).

5   Aggregate data on ethnicity in Indonesia are not available because questions on ethnicity have been omitted since the first census after independence. Only in the 2000 census was ethnicity once again part of the questionnaire. The results of the 2000 population census show that in East Kalimantan the local Dayaks comprise fewer than 10%, while the Javanese comprise 30%, the Bugis 18%, the Banjar 14% and the Kutai 9%.

6   A young local NGO leader in Samarinda, however, argues that this Forum represents the aspirations of a few in the elite, not those of the common people in East Kalimantan.

7   The regional autonomy or decentralisation statutes, Laws 22 and 25 of 1999, came into effect in January 2001 and were revised in 2004. They channelled and gave 'administrative form to a shift of power to the local level that took place soon after the collapse of the New Order in May 1998' (Aspinall & Fealy 2003:9).

8   In the case of East Kalimantan, it is interesting to note the role of Syaukani, a Kutais and district head (*bupati*) of Kutai-Kartanegara—a rich natural resources area. In the post-Soeharto era, Syaukani became an important local leader and strong advocate of real autonomy for the district government. His political influence, bolstered by his chairing the Association of District Governments in Indonesia (Asosiasi Pemerintahan Kabupaten Seluruh Indonesia or APKASI), at one time threatened the role of the governor. He had the central government in his sights, as he and his organisation became strong opponents of the central government's plan to revise the regional autonomy laws. The revision went ahead in 2004. In 2007, Syaukani was convicted and jailed for involvement in corruption cases (between 2000 and 2005) in relation to several big development projects in Kutai-Kartanegara, including the construction of an international airport in Kutai-Kartanegara. This highlights the danger some observers saw of autonomy possibly leading to 'growing corruption in local government and politics' (Aspinall & Fealy 2003:5).

Land, labour and liminality: Florenese women at home and abroad

Penelope Graham

Introduction

Land to people in eastern Flores, Indonesia, is not just a place to reside. Oral narratives that recount the ancestors' journey to join or found a village serve as a charter for people's rights of abode and access to productive land. Such narratives enjoin ritual responsibility for the wellbeing of the community and its lands (in Lamaholot, *léwo tana*). Through that obligation to nurture the land comes the opportunity to work the fields and the hope of living off the harvest. Thus, collective ritual responsibility toward the community and its lands in the eyes of Divinity and the ancestors is intimately bound up with fragile livelihoods in which land has long been and continues to be a primary economic resource. Here and elsewhere in the Austronesian world, as Thomas Reuter (2006:12) notes, such collective rights and obligations do not preclude the fact that 'as individuals with a strategic interest in a political economy based on agriculture, people also have a concern for dividing and controlling land'.

This chapter addresses issues arising for women of eastern Flores, who face traditional constraints on access to land for cultivation despite the ritual roles and responsibilities allocated to them. I explore these issues through a consideration of the tension between alternative possibilities: life at home in the ritual community and life abroad seeking wage labour in Sabah. In the 1990s, as Indonesians became even more mobile than before, their movements grew 'more complex in their spatial patterning' and mobility involved 'a wider spectrum of the population' (Hugo 1997:100). As part of this wider spectrum, an increasing number of village women joined their menfolk to travel from eastern Flores, Indonesia, to work in the Malaysian state of Sabah on the island of Borneo.[1] Developed over six decades now, this aspect of the regional labour market had remained largely unregulated until recent times, when programs developed for the control and expulsion of migrant workers were more fully implemented by Malaysian authorities, culminating in the tragedy of Nunukan.[2]

The direct and indirect participation of women from eastern Flores in this predominantly circular migration to Malaysia has an impact on their lives in a diversity of ways. As Arjun Appadurai (1991:192) has argued, more generally,

> This is not to say that nowhere are there relatively stable communities and networks of kinship, friendship, work, and leisure, as well as of birth, residence and other filiative forms. But it is to say that the warp of these stabilities is everywhere shot through with the woof of human motion, as more persons and groups deal with the realities of having to move or the fantasies of wanting to move.

To begin this chapter, I highlight a range of human impact arising from labour migration over the decades that Florenese men and women have gone to work in Sabah. I then outline the evolving gendered division of labour and local forms of access to village land in eastern Flores. This allows me to consider women's changing circumstances, as time-honoured ritual roles of 'liminal' potency in collective rites give way to mundane forms of privation at home and abroad. The discussion notes the alternative perspective that the feminisation of labour migration allows women from Flores, at least while working in Sabah, to take a more significant role as economic actors in the cash economy, with all the possibilities that entails.

My argument is that patterns of circular migration by men and women from Flores to Sabah do offer village women novel economic opportunities for wage labour, but also expose them to fraught modes of being as undocumented workers abroad and abandoned 'widows' at home. As undocumented workers in Sabah, they face the prospect of effective capture by employers and detention as well as deportation by Malaysian authorities. At the same time, a woman left behind in the village as a migration 'widow' has no access in her own right to clan land for cultivation and, in the absence of her husband and sons, must often rely on the generosity of her natal family menfolk. This lack of direct access to land may not bother those younger women for whom a significant attraction of labour migration is precisely its promise of relief from arduous labour in the fields at home. Jobs abroad are not, however, necessarily as glamorous nor as enduring as these young women may hope.

Attending Catholic church services provides Florenese migrant workers with a welcome opportunity to meet other villagers and get news from home, although such occasions may be limited to Easter and Christmas for those working on plantations or in timber mills in the interior of Sabah. In Flores, non-government organisations are taking up the issues facing migrant workers and their families. Yet without a concerted effort to find common ground between the Sabah employers who need workers and the Malaysian authorities who round up 'illegals', Florenese migrant workers remain between a rock and a hard place. They continue to develop their church networks for social solidarity abroad, and they draw on NGO health, sexuality and HIV-awareness programs for families of migrants and potential migrants in Flores. Meanwhile, labour migration 'widows' must rely on the mercy of male relatives to gain access to fields for cultivation, as they await the development of gender-inclusive land-distribution practices in the villages at home.

Stories of labour migration, life and loss in Flores

Living in a rural community in eastern Flores,[3] in the mid- to late 1980s, I was sometimes awoken at night by the unmistakable sound of a bus straining to climb the rocky, unpaved road to the village. The community in which I lived was not particularly isolated. Indeed by Florenese standards it was easily accessible, serviced daily by a mini-bus picking up villagers who wanted to go to market in the nearby port-town, Larantuka. But the sound of a large bus climbing up to the village in the middle of the night was something entirely different, as were the possibilities to which it alluded. Everyone knew this sound signalled that whomever had chartered the bus must be returning home from labour migration far, far away. The tension in the air increased as the bus drew nearer.

As an outsider, I was one of the few women in the village who could listen with equanimity to the sound of the bus straining in the dark. Most village women had husbands or sons, fathers or brothers who might be returning on that bus. Soon after its revving roused people from sleep, an exited cry '*Merantau olin!*' (traveller returning) would rend the air and echo around different sections of the village. As children dashed to meet the bus and drowsy adults came tumbling out of their houses, I used to wonder how variously-placed village women experienced the long wait for that bus to arrive and disgorge its contents. Not all local women could have great hopes stirred by this peculiarly promising sound. There were men, after all, who had left the village over 30 years ago, and expectations of their return had worn pretty thin. One such man was said to be living a dissolute life, when last seen in Sabah, unable to resist the temptations of gambling and/or womanising. Local speculation was that he may be too ashamed to return to the village, embarrassed by not having much to show from his extended sojourn overseas.

Another early migrant had a brush with death twice while seeking work in Sabah. He and his brother were among a group of village men who took passage aboard a local sailing boat setting out from the neighbouring island of Adonara and heading for the east coast of Borneo. Unbeknownst to them, this was the era of President Sukarno's opposition to the 1963 formation of the Federation of Malaysia that linked the Malay Peninsula and the former British states of northern Borneo. Indonesia had adopted a policy of belligerence and confrontation toward the new political entity. As a result, the boat on which the Florenese men were sailing could not get through to the Malaysian state of Sabah, and had to turn back seeking a landing place along the cost of Indonesian Borneo (Kalimantan). By this time, the Florenese had run out of food and water. The Florenese men were undernourished and weak towards the end of the long journey, to the extent that my informant's brother succumbed and died before the boat was able to put ashore. His body was let overboard at sea. Years later on a subsequent trip, the surviving brother was working in Sabah when he was told he must be hospitalised for a serious operation. Although he knew the medical facilities on hand in Sabah surpassed what was available to him in his own country, this man chose to abandon his work abroad and travel back to Flores so he could have his surgery at home. His main concern, he said, was that should he die, he wanted to ensure his wife and children in the village would at least know of his fate, rather than being left unaware of his demise in a strange land from which he simply never returned.

Yet another migrant from the village did suddenly arrive back from Malaysia empty-handed in the late 1980s, after an absence of nearly three decades. He had worked as a bus driver and lived in Kuala Lumpur, facilitated by a Malaysian identity card, be it fake or real, that he had acquired at some stage. While driving, this man had caused an accident in which someone was killed. As a result, he was motivated to return to Flores in order to request that village elders perform a Lamaholot rite[4] for the cleansing of homicides. The rite aims to 'push away the blood' (*odo mei*) of the deceased that is otherwise understood to bring misfortune to the person who has caused the death. This man's relatively brief return to the village was thus something of a respite for him, during which he sought a ritual means to resolve troubles plaguing him elsewhere.

Other long-term labour migrants might arrive back in the village after an extended absence, just for a social visit. Sometimes such a man would be accompanied by his Malaysian wife and children, apparently to the surprise of his parents and siblings and even though the village woman to whom he was betrothed when he went away was still waiting for him. Or to be more precise: perhaps, as some said, she had been obliged to wait by the man's clan brothers, who had after all contributed to the bridewealth that secured her fecundity on his behalf. Given a cultural paradigm in which only parenthood confers true adult status, a woman's loyalty in these matters, whatever its source, might cost her dearly if her child-bearing years slipped away as she waited.

Determined perhaps to avoid this same fate, younger women whose lovers left for Malaysia promising to return soon with funds to build a solid independent house, sometimes gave up waiting and began another relationship all too soon. In one such case, the young male migrant worker did exactly as he had promised, and having saved a good deal of his Malaysian earnings made a prompt return from Sabah after less than two years away. He was mortified to find that shortly before his arrival home the woman he intended to marry had conceived a child by another man. Despite her confessing regret at her actions and rapidly arranging a termination of the pregnancy, he steadfastly refused her and soon chose to marry someone else.

During the 1970s, 1980s and 1990s, young women in the village frequently faced the experience of carrying a baby to term and giving birth without the assistance, financial or otherwise, of the child's father. Indeed, as soon as a couple's first child was conceived many a young father-to-be would leave for Malaysia for a period of two to three years. If a young mother were to lose an infant or toddler in these circumstances, she would be further distressed by the fact that the father had never seen the child and sometimes even apprehensive that he may suspect the child was not properly cared for in his absence. During my time in the village, I was on one occasion asked to take photos of a young mother grieving at her child's funeral and mortuary rites in order to provide her with a powerful visual record of events that she could set aside for the child's absent father. Indeed, the young father later thanked me for making the death of his first-born child available to him through this photographic record.

None of these summary accounts of diverse human experience is intended to address in any general sense the merits or otherwise of labour migration for people of the village. These human predicaments do, however, remind us that where circular labour migration has become a way of life for rural people, there is always a considerable cost in human terms alongside any economic gains. In stressing the indeterminate nature of the impact of this international labour migration, I am pointing to the divergent assumptions local people make about the likely result of a sojourn abroad, given how varied are the outcomes they have witnessed in the experience of their fellow villagers.

Institutional interests at different levels of church and state also generate divergent views and conflicting policies based on what officials in particular hierarchical settings perceive as the hidden dangers of and/or the benefits that accrue to such transnational labour migration. Whatever the policies formulated at the national level in Indonesia, two prominent institutional discourses promulgated locally in Flores were firmly against the patterns of labour migration established early on. A long-standing anxiety over competing codes of sexual morality informed the Catholic church's expressed concern about the adverse effects of labour migration on Christian family life in Flores. Political issues to do with the desire for order and control informed the discourse of Indonesian officials of the East Flores regency to the effect that unregulated labour migration was undermining local attempts at economic development.

Tales of working away, illegality and exploitation in Sabah

In some respects, of course, Indonesian regency officials were right to be concerned about the invisibility entailed in irregular entry to Malaysia and people's vulnerability to exploitation flowing from a lack of 'legal' status. To indicate the broader dimensions of the problem and the number of village communities involved in eastern Flores, I note that Indonesia was estimated to have almost a million 'clandestine workers' abroad by 1995, including 350,000 in Sabah and Sarawak, the two Malaysian states on the island of Borneo (Hugo 1997:75). As Florenese going to Sabah generally pass through the Indonesian province of East Kalimantan, a more specific estimate is that provided in a newspaper from that area of Borneo (*Suara Kaltim*, 23 July 1992) which considered there were about 23,000 people from eastern Flores in Malaysia in 1991.[5] According to this report, labour migration between Flores and Sabah had been going on since the 1940s, with many people arriving for family visits, but then availing themselves of work since it was so easy to find. Labour shortage was a long-standing problem, as attested by the chairman of the North Borneo Planters' Association in 1940, when he said in Beaufort, 'the present labour position is bad and is getting worse', a situation which continued through the 1960s (Tregonning 1965:154).

While the territory had a 'crying need' for labour at least from the beginning of the British North Borneo (Chartered) Company administration in 1881, the national government that came to power in 1946 soon faced an additional problem in sourcing labour. As Tregonning (1965:129) explained:

> In post-war North Borneo, there is again a shortage, and the national government faces a difficulty in remedying the deficiency that never confronted its predecessor, which always had the vast reservoir of China to tap...the Chartered Company twisted and turned to various sources with indifferent success in its efforts to augment its scanty population. In the end it was always China on which it relied. Now this supply is barred by the bamboo curtain of communism, and the national government must solve a problem, that of a non-Chinese labour pool for North Borneo...

Older men of the village in which I lived in Flores talked of entering Malaysian Borneo from the 1950s onwards, if not on the sailing boats of eastern Indonesian seafarers (Adonaranese or Bajau), then embarking from

Kalimantan on what they called a 'smuggle boat'. They also talked of receiving no pay at all month after month as they worked away on plantations in Sabah, only to find that identity papers supposedly being organised for them never materialised. Employers told them that their salaries were being paid directly to the labour contractor who had brought them to the plantation and claimed that the migrant workers owed him up to six months salary. He demanded this payment either on the grounds that he had helped them cross the border and got them the work, or that he purported to be dealing with the Malaysian authorities on the workers' behalf to regularise their employment status and get them official papers. While some episodes recounted to me refer to the early days of irregular labour migration of Florenese to Sabah, practices of 'bonded labour with no clear accounting ever being kept of the debt that the worker has incurred' (Jones 1995:6) remain commonplace in the systemic exploitation of Indonesian labour migrants in Malaysia.

At least one man from the Florenese village I lived in decided that since he could not put up with this debt bondage, which seemed to go on indefinitely, he would simply abscond and take his chances beyond the plantation with neither papers nor funds. He ended up in what he described to me as a Malaysian jail, but which may have been one of the detention centres specifically for illegal immigrants.[6] In any case, he was then expelled across the border into Indonesian East Kalimantan upon his release. If conditions for illegal immigrants awaiting deportation in Sabah were anything like those in the detention centres on the Malay Peninsula, this man's account of suffering worse than anything he experienced in the annual 'month of hunger' preceding the harvest in Flores makes sense. Activists with at least one Malaysian NGO have attracted the wrath of the authorities for claiming that illegal immigrants were dying of malnutrition and/or maltreatment in government detention centres on the Peninsula.[7]

The dangers of detention for women are highlighted in the diplomatic row that erupted after a 13-year-old homeless Malaysian girl was mistakenly detained along with thousands of Filipinas during a Malaysian action against illegal immigrants. After being deported to the Philippines, the girl claimed that she had been raped by police in a Malaysian detention centre. Her case gave rise to a diplomatic protest by the Philippine president Gloria Arroya before the girl was recognised as a Malaysian citizen and escorted on a flight back to Malaysia by a Philippine official (BBC 2002).

While many Florenese have been held in detention centres in Sabah, the women I know were generally more fortunate than the Malaysian girl, having benefited from chain migration contacts that had gradually been established by earlier waves of male labour migrants. By the time women joined the migration stream from Flores to Sabah, they were mostly travelling in the company of groups of village men (husbands or clansmen), at least some of whom had usually made the trip before and were therefore aware of its perils and pitfalls. Many such women were going to join menfolk (usually brothers or husbands) already settled there. Nevertheless, not all the Indonesian women who travel to Malaysia with the intention of joining loved ones actually manage to meet up with those they seek.[8]

My reading of the Indonesian and Malaysian press on the subject of 'illegal immigrants' in Sabah suggests that the dangers for women in this clandestine migration are very real. Reports describing the influx of illegal immigrants as one of the biggest problems facing both the state and the federal governments in Sabah note that periodic sweeps result in the detention of foreign women involved in prostitution rounded up from various hotels and lodging houses (*Borneo Post* 23.9.1995).[9] It would seem the perils of labour migration for women recruited from Indonesia to travel to Sabah also include the possibility of being held captive in brothels in seedy hotels in Tawau, the port of entry from East Kalimantan (Jones 1996:18).

Malaysian newspapers report various incidents of this kind and I think we can safely assume the episodes that come to such public notice are indicative of more widespread abuses against women labour migrants in Sabah. At least some labour recruiters in Malaysia provide workers to a wide range of industries and are reported as allocating women workers to jobs of various kinds, depending on the demand. So of a group of women who arrive at about the same time, most may be sent to plantations, with some placed in domestic service, while others may quite unexpectedly find themselves set to work in brothels (Jones 1996:17). The Balikpapan-based newspaper *Manuntung* carried reports through 1994 and 1995 of Indonesian women falling prey to traffickers. Such women may be enticed with promises of good jobs and good wages working for Malaysian citizens, only to find themselves working as prostitutes in Sabah nightclubs (see, for example, *Manuntung* 29.3.1994; 10.8.1995).

If, however, villagers in Flores require substantial sums of money, they do consider that a trip to Sabah seeking wage labour is the most likely way of finding the necessary cash. Single men and married men, either alone or possibly accompanied by their families, would make their way to Malaysian Borneo. Usually stopping in Sabah, some would travel on to Sarawak, perhaps across to Kuala Lumpur or over yet another national border to Brunei. Since the late 1970s, single women have increasingly joined in this stream of people heading for 'Tawau'. In Sabah, Florenese men work primarily in timber mills and on plantations as field-hands. A few develop skills as mechanics, truck drivers or other heavy-vehicle operators. While the men are usually full-time wage labourers living in squatter settlements or on plantations, women are often employed on a seasonal basis as day-labour field-hands or else on a needs basis as cooks, washer-women, child-carers or household helpers for Sabahans. Over time, more and more Florenese have moved on from enterprises in the interior or on the east coast to take up residence in the capital, Kota Kinabalu.

A common aim of Florenese labour migrants is to save enough to repay their borrowed travel funds and return home able to construct a brick house with a corrugated iron roof and possibly even a concrete floor. Some achieve this aim, others do not save anything, and a few never return at all. During the 1970s, 1980s and 1990s, a significant number of Lamaholot men established, for a decade or more, a pattern of circular migration that saw them return to the village for short stays with their family every few years. In one such instance, an older man was joking about his son having adopted this lifestyle. It amounted, he said, to a new means of conforming to the local ideal for family planning by spacing one's children at a minimum of two-year intervals. This circular migratory pattern has serious implications, of course, not only for the men who go, but for the women and children they leave behind in the villages of Flores and the adjacent islands of the Solor archipelago (Solor, Adonara and Lembata). By one estimate, labour migration of young and able-bodied men to plantations in Malaysia from the island of Lembata had by the early 1990s 'resulted in the proliferation of female headed households' and a female to male gender ratio in some villages of 10:1 (Galuh 1991:1).

Over the last decade, some NGOs in eastern Flores have run programs in village communities on issues to do with labour migration. At one such workshop in the late 1990s, a group of young women were engaged in a discussion of what motivated girls their age to want to go to work in Sabah. The explanation that one young woman put forward was:

> There are two kinds of young men here in Flores: those who are 'with it' [*ikut mode*] and those who aren't. Those who are 'with it' all go to Sabah, so we want to go too.

Without any lengthy exegesis, it is clear that this young woman knew what she wanted: of the two kinds of young men she identified in her community, she was attracted to those who had 'get up and go'. While this statement drew laughter and smiles of recognition from all those present, it may well have encompassed more complex desires the young woman harboured for the kind of life she was seeking for herself.

When a year or two later I spoke with another young woman, whom I knew from the same village but on this occasion bumped into in Kota Kinabalu, I heard another version of what attracts young people from Flores to seek their fortune abroad. I'll call her 'Mary'. When I asked Mary what she was doing in Sabah, she hesitated. '*Guru*', interjected the young man accompanying me and I nodded, as indeed he and Mary both had family members who were teachers in Flores. Then they laughed and the joke was on me, as Mary quickly said no, no, no, she wasn't a teacher. But she did not tell me her occupation. In fact, she said, she 'did not care what she did, so long as it did not involve holding a hoe'.

I should not have been surprised at this emphatic rejection of working in the fields, as the young man had said something similar about his own situation. As a boy he was considered fortunate when he got the opportunity to leave the village to board at a good secondary school, but like others who completed that level of education, he found adjusting to work in the fields was difficult on his return. When home on school holidays, such boys would be chided by their elders in the village for having developed 'soft hands' from all that book learning. Now, a decade later, this young man told me that in Sabah he was receiving excellent training as a motor mechanic. When I asked if he liked the work, he said that he did: what he did not like, he proffered, was working in the fields or anything else that entailed baking in the hot sun.

This reminded me that after returning to Australia from my doctoral research in Flores in the late 1980s, I mentioned to an economist who specialised in Indonesia that young high-school graduates in places like Flores did not want to spend their lives growing crops in village fields. 'Well, they have to,' came the reply, 'they have no choice'. But educated young people from Flores clearly do not agree with this pronouncement, and some have gone to great lengths to seek alternative life paths.

So how does this pattern of labour migration interact with local ideas about gender and work? And are previously established gendered divisions of labour being transformed at home or abroad in the light of these changing circumstances?

Lamaholot birthing rites: evolving gendered divisions of labour

As part of birthing rites, Lamaholot villagers present the newborn with tools of trade: baby girls are shown miniature cotton-working and weaving implements, while baby boys get a small hunting-bow and a wooden replica of a spear. These are, however, deliberately anachronistic ritual evocations that suggest a far more static conventional model of gendered work than is presently the case. Contemporary Lamaholot work practices are, I would argue, rather indicative of an evolving, dynamic and experiential gendered division of labour.

The culturally conventional model to which birthing rites allude has women's productive and reproductive tasks focused on child-care, household provisioning (including barter trade) and the processing of home-grown cotton into woven textiles for clothing and exchange. Although subsumed here in the notion of provisioning the household, a great deal of rural women's time is actually spent on associated activities: gathering firewood, fetching water, picking vegetables, husking rice and feeding pigs.[10] As well as exchanging mostly tubers for the salt processed by women living on the coast, upland village women also barter and sell garden produce at the weekly coastal market. Some women stoke the fire all day beneath their husband's lontar-juice still and then sell, wholesale or retail, the resulting palm wine. Often widows or other impecunious women act as retailers on behalf of these producers. They could sell the palm wine surreptitiously at the local market, a practice proscribed within the regency in the mid 1980s, or deliver it door to door 'on subscription' to regular customers in the urban environs of Larantuka. Otherwise, villagers of all ages (but especially women) in need of cash for school fees and consumer items might spend long days piling up rocks from the dry river bed on village land near the south coast. These rock piles are then sold to road-makers and other construction contractors throughout the dry season.

Local textile production was, and still is, culturally prestigious women's work. Indigo dyeing is generally done on an individual basis. The more exacting red dye work is usually carried out by a group led by a highly-skilled woman. In the paired phrases once used to refer to adolescents' mastery of essential productive tasks preliminary to courting and marriage, women's textile work (*néket tané*) is set alongside men's garden work and lontar-tapping (*ola heré'*). These ritual language characterisations sum up the complementary productive activities of each sex in a specifically local division of labour. This juxtaposition, while apt in its own way, may or may not have ever adequately characterised the situation, but in any case it certainly does not suffice now. Indeed, I spoke with many women of all ages about this in the course of interviews to collect basic census and socio-economic data in the village. Only one elderly woman responded in these conventional terms to my inquiry about the women of the household's involvement in garden work. 'Women don't work gardens,' she corrected me sharply, as if she were offended by the suggestion. 'Even nowadays?' I asked. 'Well,' she hesitated, 'not unless they have to because their man is dead or away in Malaysia'.[11]

Leaving aside the development of labour migration, in former times men's productive lives revolved around breeding livestock (goats and pigs), hunting game, tapping lontar palms, and working swiddens. Between the two world wars, the yearly round of subsistence activities might have extended to distilling palm wine and trading it some distance away, even as far as the town of Maumere. Until fairly recently, limited outbreaks of local warfare constituted another crucial male activity. Warfare might occur between communities (and according to historical narratives between clans or peoples) as a result of arguments over missing livestock, the fixing of land boundaries, access to water sources, and treatment of women. Even nowadays, communities in dispute over crucial or shared resources, like land and water, may come close to outright hostilities at times.

A major and continuing transition in eastern Flores is the move into village cultivation of a variety of cash crops. The kinds of work entailed usually involve both men and women. This is a key strategy in government-sponsored efforts to promote local paths to development through diversification and commercialisation of the economy away from its subsistence crop base. The promotion of cash crops has provided further impetus for government-induced changes to land tenure and cropping regimes. By the late 1980s the village was well on the way to replacing shifting cultivation on clan land with separate household gardens on fixed fields. Partly in response to these changes, women have become increasingly involved in agricultural work, either assisting their menfolk or else in their own right as actual or metaphoric widows. In such cases, gaining access to land in fields has become a crucial subsistence concern for women as well as for men.

Léwoléma land rights: devolving gendered access to resources

While land and labour, essential to a subsistence economy, were once located within clans, this situation has been changing gradually over the last five decades. A clan's oral history encodes its claims with respect to rights on or access to land in ritual domains spanning a number of villages. So, for instance, the village in which I lived is one of an inter-related set of communities constituting an overarching domain known as the 'five villages' (Léwoléma). Clan narratives articulate relationships established over time between certain areas of land and particular clan segments concentrated in different communities. Thus, rights to work agricultural land within Léwoléma are based on precedence, as memorialised in the oral histories of the clans that recount their arrival and subsequent interaction in the domain.

By these means and within the area generally recognised as comprising the agricultural land worked by a given village, specific clans had rights over numerous delineated fields (*néwa*) of between one and two hectares. A number of adjacent *néwa* fields formed a single, named swidden (*etan*). Each year one swidden was opened for cultivation, while the others were ideally left fallow. Clan rights to such fields usually rest on oral historical consensus that clan ancestors originally cleared the primary forest from that land and were the first to cultivate it. Otherwise, clan rights over the fields may have been acquired from the first cultivators, when clan ancestors provided them with an elephant tusk or sacrificial animal that they needed for some ritual or exchange obligation.

By the period between the two world wars, most clans resident in the village had apparently acquired some (more or less extensive) field rights in its various swiddens, although the clans' man–land ratios were by no means uniform. Every year, when the decision was taken to open a specific swidden, the elder of each clan would allocate places in the clan's *néwa* fields within that swidden to male clan members. Clans with an excess of land in the swidden over available manpower would invite men of other clans, generally their sisters' husbands, to work the clan fields with them on a purely crop-sharing basis. In this way, each clan *néwa* was worked co-operatively by up to four men, who were usually clan members, and their wife-taking affines (*opu*). After the harvest, the produce of each *néwa* field was divided evenly among the men who had worked it.

According to one male clan elder, villagers might also work small plots of land on a fixed-field basis (*netak*) for up to ten years at a time. This was on land cleared by clan forebears, apart from the named swiddens and adjacent to similar plots worked by clansmen. These small gardens allowed householders to cultivate quick-growing vegetables or tubers for immediate consumption. They also favoured some items not generally planted in swiddens, such as slow-yielding fruit trees like coconuts or mangos. During the last five decades, this type of (semi-)permanent garden has become increasingly popular in conjunction with cash crops and the division of clan-based landholdings. In short, much clan land has now been subdivided into male householder plots, allocated to individuals by the head of each clan.

This distribution of the village's clan lands among male affiliates began in the 1950s. First, the village elders decided to thwart continuing encroachment on their land from a village of a neighbouring domain. They did this by parcelling the vulnerable area into strips of land for permanent farming and allocating one to each village male over 16 years of age. In the 1960s the local government, promoting fixed fields and cash crops, began measuring the strips of land already parcelled out. For an administrative fee, they provided the owners with certificates of title. Some strips of land changed hands, simply relinquished to anyone who could pay the fee for title, before this scheme was abandoned because of a re-organisation of local government structure. By the mid-1960s, in response to government exhortation, village elders agreed to open permanently the swidden adjoining these individually held strips of land. This swidden was farmed in the usual way, but after the harvest each *néwa* field was divided among the four men who had worked it that year for continuous fixed-field gardening. This practice gradually caught on in a number of adjacent swiddens. By the mid 1970s, village clans had thus divided all their lowland holdings among their adult male affiliates. During the 1980s, further allocations of clan land extended this process into the village's highland swiddens. All village land is now technically divided among male householders on a de facto basis, although at least through the 1980s some of it was still being worked by the elders as swiddens in rotation considered essential to the ritual regulation of the agricultural cycle.

Clans as corporations share interests in more than just land. Long before this recent commodification of land, some conversion between forms of capital took place both within and between clans. Thus, clan rights in *néwa* fields might be acquired through providing a much needed elephant tusk or sacrificial animal to another clan. In a good year, part of the harvest could be sold to merchants from Larantuka or Maumere to acquire an Indian trade textile or an elephant tusk to add to the clan's store of wealth and prestige. Or a portion of the clan members' rice crop might be set aside, as was done by one village clan in the 1950s and 1960s, for lending on a 'return two for every one borrowed' basis to less fortunate villagers. This particular enterprise provided the finance for that clan's male elders to build the first group of brick houses in the village. By the 1980s, the same clan had sold its elephant tusks and *patola* cloths not considered essential for clan ritual. It did so in order to establish a cash reserve from which its younger members could borrow to finance their initial labour migration transport costs. This was explicitly described to me, by one of the leaders of the middle generation of the clan, as converting resources to a new form of capital more appropriate to the contemporary era.

This sketch of changing social and economic circumstances in the village allows me to draw attention to certain aspects of the relationship between clans as corporations and men and women. With the gradual shift from clan rights over swidden fields to adult male rights over garden plots, people residing together in a household rapidly became the unit of production as well as the locus of consumption. This change opened the way for women to become agricultural producers beside their menfolk, but it also highlights the difference between men's and women's rights in clan resources. In the 1980s, unmarried women worked alongside their fathers and brothers on the land these men acquired from their natal clan. Married women, living with their husband of another clan, worked alongside their husband and sons on the land acquired from that clan. Women who were spinsters, separated or widowed could establish independent households, but they still had no access to agricultural land in their own right. Rather, they would rely on the goodwill of a man of either their natal or marital clan to allow them to borrow and work some of that man's own garden plots.

Despite some sale of clan land within and even outside the village, the differentiated relations of men and women to the productive resources of corporate clans remain fundamentally unchanged through the devolution of these resources to individuals. Some men from clans that had very little land in the village returned from labour migration then used the capital they had acquired to purchase land. So far as I know, no woman has yet attempted this. Some women were, however, utilising land allocated to a husband or son away in Malaysia, which gave them de facto access to productive resources. Spinsters and widows without continuing access through sons or husbands usually rely on the generous instincts of their brothers to gain limited access to garden plots for their subsistence and/or cash crop production. Here then, the increasing number of migration 'widows' highlights a fundamental problem in the way access to land has been devolved from clans to male householders, with women having to rely on the continuing salience of relational claims in order to gain indirect access to land.

From 'liminal' potency to privation?

In classical anthropological terms the concept of liminality refers not to an insignificant location, but rather to the central phase in a social and ritual process of transformation or renewal (Gennep 1960). The idea of being 'betwixt and between' (Turner 1969) has thus directed analysis to the potency of the (re)generative moment and the significance of the interstitial position often associated with it. While Lamaholot women hardly bear the classical hall-marks of liminality, they are ritually identified with the cyclic death and rebirth of cultivated crops, just as they are interstitial in the sociology of ideally exogamous clans. From these ritual and social positions, Lamaholot women over generations have been central to their communities both as reproducers of human life, linking the clans of 'brothers' with those of 'sisters' sons', and as a vital presence among male specialists in the ritual of the agrarian cycle to regenerate the crops that nourish human life.

As I have argued in respect of land, so in the social organisation of Lamaholot villages in eastern Flores, people have rights in and obligations to their natal clan, but these rights are fundamentally differentiated according to the sex of the person concerned. A man's relationship with the clan to which he is affiliated during his birthing rites remains relatively constant over his lifetime and beyond. The position of women with respect to clans is more complex, as analysis must take into account not only a woman's affiliation to her natal clan, but also her intense involvement with the clan of her husband and children. For most, though not all women, these will be two different clans, and the relationship with each of them at any time depends on the point a woman has reached in her own life cycle. The relationally complex position of women, who remain sisters to their natal clan even as they become wives and mothers to persons of another clan, is crucial to human reproduction in putatively agnatic lines. This vital female link is marked in ritual and celebrated in exchange relations.

So, too, in agricultural rites for the regeneration of rice and other cultivated crops, women are considered ritually akin to the annual cultigens that must go through death and rebirth in the seasonal cycle. This ritual identification of village women with the mythical rice maiden is enacted from the morning a specific clanswoman must bring the seed rice down out of the village granary, having spent the night in seclusion there. The identification continues through to the evening towards the end of the agricultural cycle when 'sisters', resuming the role of the mythical maiden from whose body these cultigens are understood to stem, accompany the newly harvested seed rice as it is ushered into the village and placed in the granary, where it will remain in seclusion until the following season. Once again, these 'sisters' spend the night seated by the rice maiden before returning to more mundane activities in the village the next day.

There were times centuries ago when the introduction of maize, rice or even earlier introduced cultigens required dramatically altered technology and work regimes for the people of eastern Flores, but offered them in return new and better modes of subsistence. A corpus of oral mythology in formalised ritual language records that such major transformations in village livelihood did not always come about smoothly or easily. Nevertheless, opportunities were seized and adaptations were made.

Given the new international division of labour that is articulating rural communities like these into global capitalism, I wonder whether the re-generative and re-constitutive fecundity of Lamaholot women will continue to evoke such notions of interstitial or 'liminal' potency. At present, more invidious modes of being 'betwixt and between' are engulfing them, since the women talk of life in squatter settlements around the towns in Sabah as if they were both politically and spiritually displaced persons there. As 'illegal immigrants' subject to employer exploitation and likely to suffer police harassment as well, one group of Lamaholot women speaking of their time in Sabah said with dismay that they were often made to 'feel like thieves'.

But as Malaysia conducts periodic drives in which politicians announce that the aim is to sweep illegal immigrants from the country, Indonesia embarks on projects to convert forms of traditional land tenure into sets of regulations for the issuing of certificates of ownership for cultivable land (*Inside Indonesia* 1996:25). In this context, the directions of change in gendered divisions of labour and the issues involved in establishing access to land for cultivation suggest the need for recognition of Florenese women, not only as wage labourers overseas, but also as independent cultivators at home. Otherwise, some Florenese women will find that their subject positions do not so much afford ritual potency, as offer only practical privation whether at home or abroad. They may then start to 'feel like thieves' living on the produce of borrowed land, not just in Sabah, but even at home in the villages of eastern Flores.

Endnotes

1   For documentation of migration flows from Indonesia to Malaysia, see Azizah
    (1991); Hugo (1993b; 1995; this volume); Kaur (2004; 2005; 2006); Pillai (1992;
    1995). For discussion of migration from eastern Flores to Sabah, see Hugo (1993b;
    2000c). For analyses of women's international labour migration from Indonesia,
    see Hugo (2002b), and in Southeast Asia, Hugo (2006d); Kaur (2007); Wee &
    Sim (2004).

2   On 1 August 2002, the Malaysian government enacted Immigration Act
    No.1154/2002 and began mass deportation of undocumented foreign workers.
    Although similar sweeps of foreign workers had been made during the 1990s,
    this was by far the largest repatriation. The sudden influx of deportees caused a
    humanitarian crisis in transit points on the Indonesian side of the border, including
    in Nunukan, a town on a small island off the coast on the East Kalimantan side of
    Indonesia's border with Malaysian Sabah (see Tirtosudarmo 2004; Ford 2006).

3   For reasons of privacy I do not name either the individual people or the particular
    local places referred to in this article. While I have tried to make my account
    specific enough to be informative and useful, similar stories could be told by
    labour migrants from many a village in eastern Flores and the adjacent islands.

4   This is one of many rituals associated with the ancestral religion of Lamaholot-
    speaking peoples of eastern Flores and the Solor archipelago.

5   I would like to thank Sidney Jones, Terence Hull and the Library of the Institute
    of Southeast Asian Studies in Singapore for sharing with me their files of press
    clippings on the issue of labour migration between Indonesia and Malaysia.

6   During one of the periodic sweeps to round-up illegal entrants into Malaysia, the
    Sabah-based *Borneo Post* (14.9.1995) reported that police lock-ups and prisons
    throughout the state were fully occupied by illegal immigrants awaiting deportation.
    In the course of that round-up, authority over the designated detention centres in
    Sabah passed to the Federal Task Force of the National Security Council, who
    were given full responsibility to monitor the influx, detention and repatriation
    of illegal immigrants from the state. Earlier, following evidence of indiscipline
    and corruption among the Police Field Force personnel running detention centres
    on the Malay Peninsula, responsibility for releasing detainees whose employers
    regularised their status passed from police to immigration officials. At the time,
    up to 80 detainees daily were being released in this way from the two centres
    (Semenyih and Lenggeng) in the Klang Valley on the Peninsula (*Malay Mail*
    2.7.1994)

7   In 1995, the Malaysian NGO Tenaganita became the subject of criminal
    investigation over its report on conditions in immigration detention centres on the
    Malay Peninsula. In a statement of concern at the prospect of Tenaganita being
    prosecuted for criminal defamation over the report, the Malaysian Bar Council
    argued that this should not be allowed to deflect attention from the government's
    admission of some 50 deaths at the Semenyih and other detention camps, nor
    from the Prime Minister's promise of an independent inquiry if necessary (*New*

Straits Times 21.9.1995). For an account of the Tenaganita case as it developed from 1996 to mid-1999, see Jones (2000:106–26).

8   The *Riau Pos* (20.8.1995), for instance, reported that of 226 Indonesian labour migrants deported from the Malay Peninsula and arriving in Dumai harbour a few days earlier, 43 were women who had gone to Malaysia seeking their husbands without success. Of those, 14 were reportedly from Indonesia's West Nusa Tenggara province and two were from the East Nusa Tenggara province that includes Flores.

9   The *Borneo Post* (12.9.1995) reported the Malaysian Deputy Home Minister as noting that a total of 668 foreign prostitutes were detained during the first eight months of that year. The women, who inclded 335 Indonesians, were said to have entered the country without valid travel documents through either the Malaysia–Thailand or the Malaysia–Indonesia border and otherwise by sea across Malaysia–Philippines waters.

10   Collecting firewood and water is so much a preoccupation of women's work that it forms a euphemism for menstruation, which women refer to as 'our work' (*gerian kamé*) or by analogy 'my water and wood' (*wai kajo go'én*).

11   I then asked 'What *do* they do?' 'Make cloths,' she replied, indicating proudly the textile she had donned to have her photo taken. For me, this sums up the status of women's textile work as a cultural ideal. In fact, since a modernisation drive by local government officials in the 1970s disrupted the customary mode of transmission of textile skills, many younger women have not mastered the full range of textile production techniques (see Graham 1994).

Crossing the threshold of home: eastern Indonesian female migrants and shifting subjectivity

Catharina Purwani Williams

Introduction

Hundreds of eastern Indonesian women pass through cramped ports, stations and terminals. They can be seen on buses, ferries and ships. The women are on the move. I followed some of their trails by sea, from the islands of Flores and Timor in East Nusa Tenggara to the urban centres of Surabaya and Makassar. Contemporary eastern Indonesian women's migration reflects the conceptual appeal of movement and crossing the threshold of home. *Langgar laut*, literally crossing the ocean, also means leaving home. This cultural and geographical threshold separates home and away, and self and other. The movement is more than a physical shifting between one geographical location or cultural experience and another. Metaphors of movement as 'imaginary trajectories' of 'here and there', 'the inside and outside', 'I and not I', are found to be strongly associated with identity (Robertson et al 1994:2). Through migration one crosses the boundaries of a space of familiarity in the midst of the unknown. Why and how do the women migrate and what does *langgar laut* or crossing the threshold of home mean for individual women? I am interested in the women's own interpretation of migration as a means to map and understand contested spaces (Tsing 1993:216), including their notions of home and away.

During my first field trip to eastern Indonesia, I met a young woman on a boat who graciously shared 'her space' on the lower deck with me. Not only did she literally give me a space on a wooden bench to sit on, but metaphorically she also created a critical space for me to start an ethnography of woman travelling, by readily sharing her stories. Her main purpose for migration, looking for opportunity, resonates with others I later met. Travel is often a metaphor for a search for a place in which happiness may be found, 'a utopian space of freedom, abundance and transparency', constituting a break or 'an inversion of everyday order' in search of new opportunities and possibilities (Curtis & Pajaczkowska 1994:199).

In Indonesia the increase in women's migration reflects the general rise in population mobility, which is linked to rising incomes, education and better communication and transport services. Women's mobility also positively

133

correlates with the participation of women in the labour market, particularly
in the fast-growing sectors of education and health services, providing sources
of mass employment (Oey-Gardiner 1997:135; Manning 1998:100, 264).
Autonomous travel by women in Indonesia (both temporary movement and
migration), unlike that by men, has been little examined until recently, as travel
is naturalised as a man's discourse. A woman's moving out of home through
migration raises an interesting issue about a need to widen the focus of the
economic reasons for migration, to include the importance of the women's
notion of place (home and away) and its link to subjectivity. Women are moving
out of the region for much richer reasons, which may not be captured by the
economic approaches to migration.

Migration research employing broad political and economic frames
dominates the work on people's mobility, mainly using neo-classical economics
and macroeconomics of development analysis associated with the 'push–pull'
factors of labour movement across regions, implying an unproblematic notion
of place (Lawson 1998:41). As Silvey and Lawson (1999) argue, within
this developmentalist perspective, migration is largely assumed to occur for
economic reasons, reflecting a Western modernisation trajectory. Women's
migration from rural to urban areas is assumed to be part of the problem of
surplus labour in the rural agricultural sector and the growing demand for
labour in industrial sectors in urban areas, leaving the possibility of other
reasons for migration unquestioned (Silvey & Lawson 1999:122–3). Feminist
scholars offer some insights into understanding the complexities of women's
migration in the form of women's ambivalent subject positions in relation to
spatial movements (Blunt 1994a; 1994b). Feminist approaches to migration
include variables such as gender, class and race as determinants of women's
mobility, as shown in an expanding set of theoretical and empirical works
on gender and mobility (see for example Bondi & Domosh 1998; Duncan
& Gregory 1999; Laws 1997; Lawson 1998; McDowell & Sharp 1997;
McDowell 1999; Pratt 1992; Yeoh & Huang 1999a). Women's mobility in
these approaches is connected with a gendered space of home; it also represents
a space at the margin of women's daily routines (Yeoh & Huang 1999b).
These approaches offer greater potential to understand East Nusa Tenggaran
women's migration to urban centres. Within this wide range of approaches,
recent works ascertain the importance of power relations in the constructed
differences of gender, ethnicity and class in shaping the experiences of
women migrants (Gibson 2001; Kofman & England 1997; McDowell 1999).
Following a more nuanced conceptualisation of power, my research explores
the specific practices of power through the spatial move or an entangling of
migration and its consequential release of power for migrants (Sharp et al

2000). Critical ethnography on women's mobility has a theoretical potential to address complex questions about women's identity and subjectivity in relation to multiple sites (Lawson 2000; Stacey 1997). This work acknowledges that places are interpreted differently between genders, so decisions on mobility are also gendered (Lawson 2000; Silvey & Lawson 1999:123).

Place, space and social relations

This research is a part of a larger study on contemporary eastern Indonesian women's travel to three types of destinations: inter-island, urban centres and overseas. The six-month field research was conducted mainly in 2000:

- in the popular migration destinations, as established by census data, including Makassar (Sulawesi) and Surabaya (Java);

- the places of origin in parts of East Nusa Tenggara; and

- while travelling on boats in the region.

A reconnaissance trip ascertained the sheer number of, and thus the focus on, women in the caring professions. For this part of the research I conducted in-depth interviews with 15 informants, seven teachers and eight nurses. Three migrants' stories are selected here to highlight the interplay of space, subject, and subjectivity of migrants. The women are originally from rural or semi-rural areas in East Nusa Tenggara, with a middle-level income, mostly with farming family backgrounds. Initial connection with a few informants generated snowballing engagements with the rest of them. We comfortably used Indonesian language for communication.

East Nusa Tenggara is a diverse region in terms of its physical geography and people. The scattered islands of the region, its hilly and mountainous areas and the dispersed small population occupying small pockets of fertile land have influenced both the traditional settlement patterns and the people's contemporary subsistence lifestyles. Difficulties in transport and communication create a sense of isolation (Jones 1995:8–14). East Nusa Tenggara province consists of 4.7 million hectares of land supporting 3.9 million inhabitants (Badan 2001:37). It is one of the least urbanised provinces in Indonesia, with less than 20% of the population living in urban areas. In the province, 65% of the population aged 10 years and over is recorded as economically active in the year 2000. The remaining 35% includes students attending school and housewives working at home (Badan 2001).

Some of the economically active women choose to work outside the region, which conflicts with the image of a domesticated, 'virtuous' woman (Williams

HORIZONS OF HOME

2003). By migrating as teachers or nurses, women are able to perform a gender role that is 'socially, historically and geographically constituted' (Laurie et al 1999:4). During my field research in Surabaya and Makassar I met many women from East Nusa Tenggara in the caring profession. I noticed how women chose to present their migration to the city as related to their function as professional carers. Teaching and nursing professions fit nicely with the expected gender role in dominant femininity, which is nurturing. The elevation of teaching and nursing professions in the local context as a 'divine calling' produces a unique mission that necessitates travel for women as part of their 'vocation'. Why do women use this path to leave home?

The history of romantic travels within the West—begun in the late 18th century and lasting until the end of the 19th century—repeats itself within journeys of contemporary East Nusa Tenggaran women travelling for *panggilan* or 'vocation'. One of the central goals of romantic travel is to be immersed in cultural difference (Duncan & Gregory 1999:8)—and this resonates with my informants' wish to travel to urban centres. They too seek an experience of difference from their home of rural or semi-rural origin, and this curiosity is framed by a romanticising of their motives as being those of caring for others. The availability of teaching and nursing jobs in the cities facilitates the flow. However, women's agency is as important as the economic structure in directing them towards the feminised occupations (Bozzoli 1991:967). The elevation of these caring professions in the local context has been amplified by the state's ideology manifested in the dominant femininity. Whilst it constrains their mobility in some ways, the dominant femininity has been reproduced and successfully used by the women as a justification for their migration. My analysis of women's migration to urban centres attempts to tease out the emerging and changing constitution of migrant subjects. To do so, I trace the ways they imagine and take up different identities outside the threshold of home.

Women's migration stories present issues that highlight the mutual constitution of changing spaces and subjectivity, enabling me to tease out the emergence of a new subjectivity among migrants leaving home. I present the context of migration from their home villages and pay attention to women's experiences that reflect ways in which women, as subjects, understand their migration to work in the feminised caring professions. I argue that women take advantage of 'patriarchal bargains' rather than challenge social structures, as active agents moving out of home to achieve personal goals, which enable shifting subjectivity (Kandiyoti 1998; Sharp et al 2000).

Leaving home: beyond boundaries

Individuals often simultaneously support some aspects of social order, such as patriarchy, whilst opposing others. Migrants' spatial movements from home convey the complexities of adopting feminine employment to break free of the confines of gendered expectation at home. I conceptualise these women's experience as a 'repositioning of self' (Pile & Thrift 1995:201).

Rural women who migrate to urban centres embody both physical and metaphorical movement, which fits with a notion of crossing the boundary or threshold of home:

> Every voyage can be said to involve a re-siting of boundaries. The travelling self is here both the self that moves physically from one place to another, following 'public routes and beaten tracks' within mapped movement, and the self that embarks on an undetermined journeying practice, having constantly to negotiate between…a here and a there, and an elsewhere (Minh-ha 1994:9).

The women cross the threshold of home via different spaces. They negotiate a range of boundaries as defined by the spatiality of home. The journey of migrants creates a transient space, where the rules are blurred, and recreates the migrants' notions of space where they feel at home.

Feminist analysis requires attention to place-based identities and relationships within spatial and historical contexts (Domosh and Morin 2003:258). The relational nature and material cultures of the women's everyday lives reveal gender as embodied and discursive (Jacobs and Nash 2003:265). Here I focus on gendered boundaries of propriety under the dominant femininity that structure local relations in East Nusa Tenggara.

Historically, young men from certain coastal localities migrate. In the pre-colonial period, men's domain of mobility such as trade and other localised interaction, including migration, was conducted along inter-island routes.

> The ancestral migrations and early exchanges of goods and know-how are memorialized in mythic form by many people of Flores, who regard knowing and respecting their origins as crucial to their contemporary survival. Such myths and historical accounts often depict Flores not as a bounded entity, but in relation with various 'outsiders' (Graham 1999:72).

In contrast, women's spatial movement is mostly related to their domestic role in the household. During my fieldwork, I saw women of Kédang (Lembata Island) spending significant amounts of time walking considerable distances (up to two hours twice daily) to fetch water from springs. I also observed the labour intensive activities of preparing food for the family, beginning with the lighting of fires first thing in the morning. During the day eastern Indonesian women spend long hours and exert hard physical labour in producing hand-loomed textiles and other domestic activities. Three strong material symbols—water, firewood and loom—stand out among others to represent gender roles and local femininity. Water and firewood signify women's work to provide food and other services for the household. The loom signifies women's roles within the clan or community in upholding obligations to customary law (*adat*). The production of hand-loomed textiles (*tenun ikat*) is labour intensive, with the finest textiles used for ceremonial purposes. Women's tasks in caring for the family are naturalised at home within the gendered spaces of family and a kinship system.

Through mythical representation in the form of folk narratives, locals think of themselves in terms of their relationship with the 'other'. Migration has been a way of encountering the 'other' but it now has the added dynamic of women being included as both migrant and 'other'. Contemporary women now follow some male ancestral trails not only by sailing inter-island but also by moving transnationally to forge connections with other shores. More than just waiting for their men to come home, women also circulate, engaging in their own spatial practices. Migration to work challenges women's spatial association with home and a particular femininity (McDowell 1999); these women are thus stepping into an ambiguous contested space of female migration.

The home, where many women still derive their most important social and political roles and identities, is an important reference. Redefining their relationships within home, as well as between home and the wider community is then an important means of elaborating new strategies. As migrant women change their home in many ways they also change their way of life, their way of being, and the way of thinking connected to their identities (Harcourt & Escobar 2002:9). Home is a site of familiarity. Migration is a constructed space comprising a range of spatial practices offering a critical distance from familiarity. Distance often facilitates new perspectives. The new perspective arising from familiarity is that of seeing and knowing other places and spaces. Migration is bounded by points of departure and destination and therefore defined by perceptions of familiarity or home. In Flores, East Nusa Tenggara, home is not only closely linked to a house or dwelling that serves as a basic unit of social organisation; it is also equivalent to the identity of kin groups. It involves a source of origin that relates to a family genealogy or source of blood (Forth 1998; Tule 2004). Migration therefore involves a reworking of the personal and a 'de-familiarisation', a break and separation of the collective identities as reflected in the meanings of home and family/kin.

For the women in Flores, migration represents a reworking of their association with home. Their cultures seem to recognise that not only people but also places 'travel' (Strathern 1991); notions of home also move and shift. Through migrants' personal stories I have found that women's notions of home change with their migration. By decentring home and family women modify their behaviour, recreate their identities, and shift subjectivities, raising an important question on the essentialised association of place and identity (Elmhirst 2000; Silvey 2000). Migrants' changing notions and associations of place, including home, are apparent later in their migration accounts.

Through migration, women cross the threshold of home—the propriety frame historically used to discipline women (Jacobs & Nash 2003:267). McDowell (1999:4) argues that: 'Places are made through power relations which construct the rules which define boundaries. These boundaries are both social and spatial—they define who belongs to a place and who may be excluded.'

In migration women enter different scales of relations. My informants' stories of travel contain imagery of negotiating a macro scale of boundary, depicting eastern Indonesian identities from a periphery going to the centre of power in Java. This imagery follows the state discourses of social and economic development, in which eastern Indonesia is associated with lack. A single woman's journey also represents a negotiation of kin and a gendered boundary of propriety in decision making at the local scale. Once away, she, rather than her male kin, makes decisions, including those about her mobility. The bodily scale of boundary is also negotiated when a single young woman travels.

Migration and caring professions

A professional path as a teacher or a health worker in the context of East Nusa Tenggara commands high respect from the community. Both professions contain a 'sacred' connotation, *pekerjaan mulia*, meaning honourable job. *Ibu guru*, a reverent title for a female teacher in the villages that I visited in Ende, Flores, is one of a higher social status, similar to a *mantri* or a health worker. Thus women's choice of the socially acceptable occupation of carer in contemporary Indonesia under state *ibu-ism* (Suryakusuma 1996) becomes a perfect frame for their migration. They can still maintain the gender role of caring and extend it to the public sphere, in schools or hospitals. My field research shows that in their *kampung* (hamlets), not only do people respect women in these sacred professions, but most perceive them as virtuous women, despite their migration. Language used for these professions shows the significance of the jobs—sacred professions, *pekerjaan mulia*. Some women felt strongly that they were being 'called', *terpanggil*—the way Catholic priests or nuns are called to serve God—to take on the responsibilities of caring. The association of women and domesticity reflects maintenance of the gender roles. At the same time the status of these professions shows local possession of both knowledge and power.

The association of women with home resonates with the experiences of other women travellers in different spaces and times. Biographies and interpretation of works of individual women travellers of the West in the 19th century confirm that, despite being confined to a woman's place 'which was first and foremost at home', when a woman travelled her identity in relation to the domestic sphere was altered (Lawrence 1994:x).

I present the stories of Detti, Evi and Ima because they not only provide the observable material condition of the women's crossing the threshold of home to the urban centres, but also contain imaginative journeys of identity enabling shifting subjectivity. Through their stories I explore how women attempt to balance social expectations with their own strategies to be 'oneself', *menjadi diri sendiri*—a repositioning of self 'to feel at home within' and gain autonomy/power.

Nursing in public and in private: Detti

Detti was a single, soft-spoken nurse in her early 30s, whom I met through a friend in a hospital in Surabaya (Java). As the youngest in a family of seven children of whom all, except her, had married and left home, Detti was last in the family's hierarchy. As an unmarried daughter and a youngest sister, she was under the protection and authority of her family. This relationship reflected the hierarchical gender and kinship structure of the local community in the district of Timor Barat. Detti turned her life around, starting with her migration to the city. Her justification for leaving the village was that she was *terpanggil* or 'called' to care for others. This line of reasoning was too noble for the family to dismiss. Her decision to pursue this profession evidently subverted her typically subordinate position within her family.

Detti arrived in Surabaya to study to become a nurse ten years ago. Her most recent trip back to her home in a subdistrict of Kefamenanu in Timor Barat was the first in three years. Vaguely, she mentioned some pressures and resentment from the family about her rare visits home. The few trips back home were the product of her rational decision, where the cost of transport and other problems associated with going home, including *oleh-oleh* (gifts from travel), was high in relation to her income.

One weekend I unexpectedly stayed with Detti overnight in her tiny one-bedroom rented house in a small alley in Surabaya. It was six o'clock in the evening and beginning to get dark, and torrential rain poured down. The area was flooded, so I was stranded there. I offered to buy our dinner in a nearby flooded *warung* (small food stall), and went there by *beca* (trishaw). Kindly, Detti later invited me to share her single bed in a cramped two by two metre room, which I gratefully accepted. While busy helping her empty the buckets that were constantly filling with water that whooshed from the roof cracks, I shared a piece of Detti's everyday routine, typical of the life of a woman in the city by herself. Detti appears to be an independent professional. She expressed a strong intention to break away from her mother's life path as a local housewife, as she imagined and preferred different identities. Interestingly Detti, having renegotiated her identities and turned her back on the subject position of 'housewife' in the village, seemed to have located herself within the domestic role as a carer—a motherly figure in the city. She indicated that it was her role to be 'there' in Surabaya and to care not only for the physically sick but also 'to help anyone in need'. Not surprisingly, I witnessed her strong bond with others from the region who often visited her rented house. Her identities as a motherly and capable figure for a small group of young students from East Nusa Tenggara and a professional nurse were grounded in the local context of living in a *kampung* within Javanese neighbourhoods and working in a city's hospital. Detti attracted the affection of her community for a few good reasons. She was able to draw on her wide social network. This was an asset for the community.

While with her, I observed her reaction to an incident that unfolded before our eyes as she helped an elderly couple from her village of origin. They were on a mission from Timor to find their daughter's boyfriend in Surabaya. The young couple were students there, but the boy had disappeared after the girl confided that she was carrying his baby. Competently, Detti made arrangements for the confused family. As the youngest child, she would not usually command such authority in her own family. She took the elderly couple to her rented house, providing them with a place to stay, albeit crowded, and served them food. The couple were in obvious distress over the state of their daughter's affairs. Their daughter was perceived as 'living in a state of sin' according to their Catholic faith. By extension the parents were 'impure' and were denied Holy Communion by their local parish priest. Calmly, Detti negotiated some difficult decisions on behalf of the couple. She arranged a search for the frightened boy. He was given a 'lesson' and thus suffered bruises, but he agreed to marry the girl. By contacting the right people Detti helped to arrange for a private church marriage for the young couple. According to their local tradition there would be *adat* (customary law) to be taken care of and the young man's family would have to pay a fine in addition to the girl's bridewealth. The spatiality of Detti's intervention in the negotiation of marriage raises an interesting aspect of power, which 'can not be imagined as unidirectional or panoptic-like' (Robinson 2000:203). She was caught up between following the social order of local tradition and exercising her judgment at a time of crisis.

Her subtle leadership role in the place to which she had migrated highlights Detti's agency and the multidimentional aspects of power. As a consequence of her migration, new relations of power are established that to some extent enable and permit her power (Sharp et al 2000:24). The incident also displays the mutual constitution and performativity of spaces and identities (Blunt 1999:423; IBG 1997:196). Crossing the threshold of home, Detti emerged not only as an autonomous capable woman but also as an authoritative figure with the right connections in the community and the local church. Her relocation enabled shifting subjectivity as she moved between various identities. The multiple identities Detti occupies put her on a firm footing as an autonomous subject within her circle in the city. She used a simplistic, altruistic line to explain her move: 'It was my duty to help others. I travelled all the way here, there must be a purpose for this. There is some thing that I have to do, which is actually my "calling".'

Detti's feminine caring identity in the informal social group and as a nurse in the hospital space moved her through wider social networks to her advantage. As the story indicates, the private and public spheres of Detti's everyday life created norms and practices that produce and reproduce gendered activities and social relations within them (Martin 1992:208). Her decision to pursue her profession in the city proves that it was a strategic move. Detti feels 'at home within' as a migrant occupying wider subject positions.

Mobility and purity: Evi

Evi, an outgoing 29-year-old married nurse, gained a reputation among her peers in Surabaya as an exemplary nurse, *perawat teladan*. Originally from Flores, she was the first child of seven children of a tightly knit family of a *suku* or clan of Sikka. Evi's *langgar laut*, leaving the family home, started when she was 18 years old, when she entered the nursing school in Surabaya. However, her imaginary mobility started with a fantasy when she was barely seven years old and had wanted to go and study in Java:

> I had been wanting to be a nurse since I was a little girl. My mum was hospitalised once, when I was about seven years old and I had a direct experience of knowing the nurses who looked after her. They were lovely people in white uniforms so I was very impressed. Although I didn't know much about a nurse's duties at the time. This left a lasting impression deep in my mind,

that I would like to be like those nurses when I grew up. Ever since I could remember I had always wanted to be like them in white uniform and helping sick people...(field notes)

After completing her education, she secured a permanent job as a nurse in a reputable hospital in Surabaya. Ever since, she has travelled regularly between Surabaya and Flores. Evi's residence was in a two-storey brick house on the side of a busy road in a central area in Surabaya. Her husband worked in a private company, earning a very good income. The couple lived comfortably, as shown by their house and the modern household appliances in their home, including large television and stereo sets. The lounge room was spacious, painted in an off-white colour, three-by-four metres in size. On the wall there were two of her 1998 wedding photos, enlarged in fancy frames. The lounge chairs were comfortable, made of carved mahogany with crimson velvet upholstery, an interior style commonly found in middle-class Javanese houses in urban areas. As we sat comfortably sipping a glass of iced tea that a maid had served us, she told me her story. Her life, in her own words, was *penuh badai* (full of storm) and had its share of torments and troubles. An advantage of being away since such a young age was, *bisa menjadi diri sendiri*, to be 'at home within'. She was able to resist indirect kin and community pressure to remain in her home village until marriage.

Being away from home had consequences for her reputation. She was aware that her mobility to the city defied certain local norms of gendered propriety. Her frequent travels aroused gossip about the possibility of improper relations with men in other places. Evi's solo travels to and within urban areas created a perception at home that she was 'loose'. To migrate for work in the city is to be potentially impure, despite her caring profession. This had negatively affected her relationship with a potential spouse. The time of her courtship with her (now) husband was plagued with arguments and his jealousy. He accused her of playing around, on the basis of her mobility. In this sense her mobility was equated with freedom of the road, including sexual freedom. The polarity of purity/impurity of her body in connection with her migration appeared several times throughout her stories. Evi shared with me her internal tensions in dealing with the external perception of her femininity. Her subject position as a daughter and a member of the clan created a dilemma between on one hand, her obedience to stay within propriety boundaries and purity of her body, and on the other hand, her choice of an identity as an autonomous woman. From her comments about her community I found that she was aware of the society's double standard applied to women's purity in relation to her migration, which is not an issue for men. Evi's resistance to the double standard on purity of the body related to her mobility manifested itself in a stance against the fiancé, which resulted in a tense relationship with him. He accused her of having an affair. There had recently been repeated cases of single Florenese girls who fell pregnant, known as 'losing their virtues' after intimate relationships in the city. Evi was particularly hurt at being accused of *hilang kesuciannya*, or losing her virginity/virtue:

> I did not defend myself or make any effort to that effect, just challenged him [the fiancé] to find another girl whom he was certain was a virgin...However, he did not want to end the relationship and eventually we got married. At our wedding night he sobbed and asked for forgiveness for once doubting my virginity, as he then knew the truth (field notes).

Evi continues to negotiate between her mobility and boundaries of propriety. Other informants chose to represent their migration in terms of the dominant femininity. When asked to tell their stories, they echoed similar concerns and mostly chose a virtuous representation of rescuing the young, sick or poor. This representation fits with Wilkes' description of the romantic construction of a caring career:

> The world was a place in which wrongs could be righted, tears mended, and the proper order restored. These were the points in the narratives when speakers' accounts became quite vivid, and the women spoke with forthright passion and conviction (Wilkes 1995:242).

As women 'restoring order' how could they be 'out of order' themselves? The nurses and teachers whom I interviewed were similarly passionate in describing their *panggilan* (vocation) rather than referring to it merely as a profession. And this *panggilan* necessitated and justified their migration to urban centres. The romantic form of my informants' description of their *panggilan* was, however, contingent upon the context and sequence of the stories. Behind their migration stories there is a shared theme of how the individual is strategically distancing herself from home and the family to create a space for repositioning self and to make herself feel at home anywhere.

Most of my informants nominated an altruistic motive of 'being able to help people' as they moved to take up teaching and nursing. They presented themselves as reliant on the qualities of the dominant femininity, which also bears the footprints of the state gender ideology. This view draws heavily on the expected behaviour of *tahu menempatkan diri*, or knowing one's place—a woman's place is to nurture, even though this woman's place is an increasingly unstable and contested space in national debates. Such justified migration overcomes the social constraints of moving away from home through the patriarchal bargain. Migration opens up wider social networks in which women widen their subject positions enabling them to draw power from within the relational network. Women who were teachers or nurses could remain within the boundaries of the gendered propriety and stay relatively free to explore other identities. As Evi's experience shows, women are able to have multiple identities that are mutually constituted through and with spaces.

Teaching and becoming: Ima

Many contemporary East Nusa Tenggaran women choose to work as teachers—one among a range of social roles in urban centres in which women perform their feminine identity. Teaching jobs with security of tenure bring not only a reliable source of income but also local prestige. Women of the region have taken the opportunity of getting a teaching job in the city as a way to access knowledge and different scales of power, as the following story indicates.

Ima was a single, friendly teacher in her mid-30s, originally from Palue island, just north of Flores. She took up her teaching appointment in Makassar in 1991 and has since travelled between the two places. Her autonomous, independent lifestyle as a single professional was one aspect of her life she valued most. This dimension of power was possible because of the distance—in a liminal space—she created between herself and the family. She was passionate about her teaching role and viewed it as her life's mission. Ima enjoyed teaching in a Catholic high school in Makassar. She displayed a personal autonomy in making the decision about her future and remaining single. Distance from family, she commented, was essential to being *mandiri*, or independent. There was less family interference with her private life, or *keluarga tidak banyak campur tangan*. Being outside the home space provided a necessary environment for her to move between a range of identities and roles. She was able to make a unilateral decision of refusing an arranged marriage. Gentle as Ima might have appeared, she had defied her extended family's wish for her to get a husband of some social status.

In the local context, a single woman was thought of as *tidak laku* or not wanted—her life is seen as 'incomplete', showing her to be of a lower status. The state ideology of the dominant femininity idealises the roles of supportive wife, good mother and impeccable housewife, which produces and reproduces a stigmatised identity for a single mature woman—*perawan tua*, meaning an old maid, as observed in many parts of Indonesia. In Java, Berninghausen and Kerstan (1992:116) note a social pressure for single eligible woman to marry:

> Once a woman has been accepted into the adult community, her sphere of activities broadens considerably, even if the marriage does not last. Compared with the societal devaluation of women who remain single, divorced or widowed women are stigmatized to a much lesser degree. However, women who live alone for whatever reason are especially subject to suspicion and destructive gossip on the part of others.

Unavoidably, Ima must have attracted a fair portion of village gossip. Her physical qualities—she is of average height, slim, dark skinned with bright eyes, a dainty nose and pleasant smile, with curly black hair that was grown to shoulder length—in the local context give no reason for her to remain single. In her village of origin, Ima had transgressed the boundaries of propriety by remaining single well into her 30s. Daughters are valued for, among other things, their potential to attract a bridewealth to increase the family's social status. As far as Ima's family was concerned, her case was a lost opportunity for an alliance with a high status family. The extended family was upset, and for a period of time they refused to talk to her. By distancing herself from the family and making her own decision, she was temporarily excluding herself from the kin and family relations. Nevertheless, Ima's decision regarding her marital status prevailed. For Ima, teaching was conforming to the dominant femininity in caring for the young, but being single went against that same femininity. The question remains, how does teaching in the city provide her with power to decide her life path?

Throughout her adult life Ima conformed to the dominant femininity. However, the physical and emotional distance gained through migration allowed her to go against that very same femininity. By becoming a single professional, she defied her family's authority. Being separated from home provided her with a space that enabled a shifting subjectivity. Her personal desires were important for her. Here, migration allows a process of becoming in which she feels at home within herself.

In presenting and analysing women's migration stories I find that the trope of travel 'provides a particularly fertile imaginative field for narrative representations of women's historical and personal agency' (Lawrence 1994:20). The migration stories highlight the women's agency in accessing a space or a feeling at home for themselves. This space mutually constitutes a wider range of identities and shifting roles. In creating the physical and emotional distance, women are able to make their own decisions, instead of relying on kin, parents or a husband. Migratory travel opens up a new space of possibilities and uncertainties, enabling women's shifting subjectivity. The women's strategic moves to the city, as Ima's story shows, underlie the economic reason for finding a teaching job in the urban areas.

Crossing the threshold: a space to feel at home

The ways these teachers and nurses described their reasons for choosing the caring occupations are not new. Contingent, micro, everyday interactions strongly shape a woman's choice of sets of social roles. At the individual level of choosing a caring occupation, a woman is, to some extent, constrained by the dominant femininity. Women's agency is crucial in the decision to pursue caring jobs in the cities, providing a justification for travel. Some informants were acutely aware of the reality of the meagre salaries of nurses and teachers, whether working in the government or in private institutions. My informants' migration to urban areas seemingly conformed to the dominant discourse of the gender roles, particularly their feminine jobs as nurse or teacher. However, analysing the migration further shows that the conforming process actually generates power from within. Once gaining mobility, the women are on the path toward new possibilities.

The women similarly travel to be able to explore a sense of self or to feel at home within. Throughout the narratives, there emerged a theme of women's shifting subjectivity in their localised relations. Through the ethnography of travel I have shown tensions resulting from travel, the conflicting perceptions, thoughts and feelings, so as to draw connections between a space and distance from home, subject and identities. My informants' stories of their migration to the city reflect deeper experiences of strategically locating themselves in a polarised opposite between conforming and transgressing the dominant femininity. In the local context, similar to the early 20th century cities in Europe, women's presence in the cities might be seen as a problem because it symbolised the promise of sexual adventure, 'a problem of order' (Wilson 1991:5-6). In Indonesia, sexual adventure, excessive ambition and assertiveness for women are seen as deviations (Hatley 1997:94). Cities represent disorder and ambiguity as far as women's sexuality is concerned, but at the same time they also offer wealth and opportunity (Wilson 1991:6).

I map women migrants as subjects taking a path on which they can move through the trajectories of power, along the lines of class, gender and race (Ferguson 1999:160). I have shown their migration as a space allowing new encounters, and thus instrumental in the contestation and creation of identities. By taking new and wider subject positions, women's subjectivity is likely to shift along with experiences of multiple spaces. My informants' migration to the cities demonstrates the process of change in their subject positions and subjectivity. Their stories show how women partly sustained the local status quo of power in order to move beyond local relations into wider social relations. This shift of relations led me to think of migration as fitting the notion of a transient space, which is on the one hand full of uncertainties and on the other hand allows them to feel at home within themselves. I argue that women exploited the fluidity and multiplicity of roles and identities in this space, enabling a shifting subjectivity.

Through their migration women gain a space to manoeuvre within the interplay of local gender relations and the dominant femininity. Women's mobility in the local context is a part of the dynamic processes of working out both the meanings of place and their own identities. The local culture, as a web of socially negotiated meanings, is embedded in the process of women's travel (Marcus & Fischer 1986; Silvey & Lawson 1999:1245). Migration allows changes from the status quo of local relations to wider connections and this reflected the women's desire to gain more power through personal autonomy and independence. Feeling at home within, gaining control of their own lives might have been the women's primary, if concealed, goal of mobility in the first place, thus exposing the limitation of the economic approach to migration. Unpacking their migration and examining their mobility as spatial entangling beyond the romance of their professions demonstrates that the local notion of *langgar laut* was a significant step in creating a space to feel at home.

Glossary

ASDT	Associacao Social-Democrata Timorense (Timorese Social Democratic Association), in 1974 a pre-cursor to Fretilin, and now a political party
Clandestine Front	an underground resistance movement supporting Falintil
CNRM	Concelho Nacional da Restistancia Maubere (National Council of Maubere Resistance)
CNRT	Conselho Nacional da Resistencia Timorense (National Council of Timorese Resistance)
Falintil	Forças Armadas de Libertação Nacional de Timor-Leste (National Liberation Forces of East Timor)
Fretilin	Frente Revolucionaria do Timor-Leste Independente (Revolutionary Front of Independent East Timor)
OFWs	Oveseas Filipino Workers
RETENIL	Restencia Nacional dos Estudantes de Timor Leste (National Resistance of East Timorese Students)
UDT	União Democrática Timorense (Timorese Democratic Union)

Bibliography

Acciaioli, GL 1998, 'Bugis entrepreneurialism and resource use: structure and practice', *Antropologi Indonesia* 57.

Adams, RH 2003, *International migration, remittances, and the brain drain. A study of 24 labor-exporting countries*, World Bank Policy Research Working Paper 2069, June.

ADB (Asian Development Bank) 2004, 'Developing the diaspora', paper presented at Third Co-ordination Meeting on International Migration, Population Division, Department of Economic and Social Affairs, United Nations Secretariat, New York, 27–28 October.

Adi, R 1996, 'The impact of international labour migration in Indonesia', PhD thesis, University of Adelaide.

Aditjondro, GJ 1986, 'Datang dengan Kapal, Tidur di Pasar, Buang Air Dikali, Pulang naik Pesawat: Telaah Dampak Migrasi Suku-Suku Bangsa Sulawesi Selatan dan Tenggara ke Irian Jaya sejak Tahun 1962', Yayasan Pembangunan Masyarakat Irian Jaya, Jayapura.

Ahimsa Putra and H Shri 1989, *Minawang: Hubungan Patron-Klien di Sulawesi Selatan*, Gajah Mada University Press, Yogyakarta.

Andaya, LY 1995, 'The Bugis-Makassar diasporas', *Journal of the Malayan Branch of the Royal Asiatic Society* 68.

Anderson, Benedict 1983, *Imagined communities: reflections on the origin and spread of nationalism*, Verso, London and New York.

—— 1993, 'Imagining "East Timor"', *Arena Magazine* 4.

Anderson, Bridget 2001, 'Different roots in common ground: transnationalism and migrant domestic workers in London', *Journal of Ethnic and Migration Studies* 27(4).

—— 2003 'Just another job? The commodification of domestic labour' in Ehrenreich, E and AR Hochschild (eds), *Global woman: nannies, maids and sex workers in the new economy*, Granta Books, London.

Ang, Ien 1993, 'The differential politics of Chineseness' in Hage, G and L Johnson (eds), *Identity/community/change, Communal/Plural* 1.

Appadurai, Arjun 1991, 'Global ethnoscapes: notes and queries for a transnational anthropology' in Fox, RG (ed), *Recapturing anthropology: working in the present*, School of American Research Press, Santa Fe.

—— 2002, 'Disjuncture and difference in the global cultural economy', in Inda, JX and R Rosaldo (eds), *The anthropology of globalisation: a reader*, Blackwell, Massachusetts.

Arao, Danilo Arana 2004 'OFW remittances needed to pay foreign debt, offset deficit', *Bulatlat.com*, www.bulatlat.com/news/4-16/4-16-ofw.html, accessed 6 January 2005.

Arenas, A 1998, 'Education and nationalism in East Timor', *Social Justice*, Summer, 25(2).

Arroyo, GM 2003a, speech delivered at the ceremonial signing into law of the Act Rationalizing the Excise Tax on Automobiles and the Philippine Citizenship Retention and Reacquisition Act of 2003, Malacañang, Philippines, 29 August, www.op.gov.ph/speeches, accessed 7 January 2005.

―― 2003b, speech delivered during mass with members of the Filipino-American Community, Los Angeles, USA, 17 May, www.op.gov.ph/speeches, accessed 7 January 2005.

―― 2003c, speech delivered to a meeting with the Filipino community in Jersey City, USA, 26 September, www.op.gov.ph/speeches, accessed 7 January 2005.

Aspinall, E and G Fealy 2003, 'Introduction: decentralisation, democratisation and the rise of the local' in Aspinall, E and G Fealy (eds), *Local power and politics in Indonesia: decentralisation and democratisation*, Institute of Southeast Asian Studies, Singapore.

AUK Management Service (no date) www.auk.com.sg, accessed 17 January 2005.

Azizah Kassim 1991, 'Recruitment and employment of Indonesian workers: problems and major policy issues', ILO Inter-Country Workshop on Migrant Labour in the Plantation Industry, Kuala Lumpur, 12–17 November.

Badan Pusat Statistik Propinsi NTT 2001, *Nusa Tenggara Timur Dalam Angka*, Biro Pusat Statistik, Kupang.

Barber, PG 1997, 'Transnationalism and the politics of 'home' for Philippine domestic workers', *Anthropologica* 39.

Basch, L, NG Schiller and CS Blanc 1994 *Nations unbound: transnational projects, postcolonial predicaments and deterritorialised nation-states*, Gordon and Breach, Pennsylvania.

Bauman, Z 1992, 'Soil, blood and identity', *Sociological Review* 4.

BBC World Service 2002, 'Malaysian rape-row girl flies home', http://news.bbc. co.uk/1/hi/world/asia-pacific/, 9 December, accessed 10 December 2002.

Berninghausen, J and B Kerstan 1992, *Forging new paths, feminist social methodology and rural women in Java*, (translated by Barbara A Reeves), Zed Books, London.

Bisri, CH 1985, 'Kalola: sebuah desa yang pernah ditinggalkan banyak penghuninya' in Mukhlis and K Robinson (eds), *Migrasi*, Yayasan Ilmu-Ilmu Sosial dan Lembaga Penerbitan Universitas Hasanudin, Ujung Pandang.

Blunt, A 1994a, 'Reading authorship and authority: reading Mary Kingsley's landscape description', in Blunt, A and G Rose (eds), *Writing women and space, mappings: society/theory/space*, The Guildford Press, New York.

―― 1994b, *Travel, gender and imperialism: Mary Kingsley and west Africa*, The Guildford Press, New York.

—— 1999, 'Imperial geographies of home: British domesticity in India, 1886–1925, *Transactions of the Institute of British Geographers* 24.

Bondi, L and M Domosh 1998, 'On the contours of public space: a tale of three women', *Antipode* 30(3).

Bonnemère, P 1998, 'Trees and people: some vital links' in Rival, L (ed), *The social life of trees: anthropological perspectives on tree symbolism*, Berg, Oxford and New York.

Bozzoli, B 1991, *Women of Phokeng: consciousness, life strategy, and migrancy in South Africa, 1900–1983*, Heinemann, Portsmouth.

Breckenridge, C and A Appadurai 1989, 'On moving targets', *Public Culture* 2(1).

Brown, L (ed) 1993, *The New Shorter Oxford Dictionary*. Oxford University Press, Oxford and New York.

BSP (Bangko Sentral ng Pilipinas) 2004, *Overseas Filipino workers' remittances by country and by type of worker*, www.bsp.gov.ph/statistics/spei/tab11.htm, accessed 7 January 2005.

Carey, P 1997, 'From Netherlands Indies to Indonesia—from Portuguese Timor to the Republic of East Timor/Timor Loro Sa'e: two paths to nationhood and independence', *Indonesia and the Malay World* 71.

Carsten, J 1997, *The heat of the hearth: the process of kinship in a Malay fishing community*, Clarendon Press, Oxford.

Chalamwong, Y 2005, 'Recent trends and policy initiatives of international migration and labor market in Thailand, 2004', paper prepared for the Workshop on International Migration and Labour Market in Asia organised by the Japan Institute for Labour Policy and Training, Japan Institute of Labour, Tokyo, 20–21 January.

Chambers, Iain 1994, *Migrancy, culture, identity*, Routledge, London.

Chang, KA and JMcA Groves 2000, 'Neither "saints" nor "prostitutes": sexual discourse in the Filipina domestic worker community in Hong Kong', *Women's Studies International Forum* 23(1).

Chatterjee, Partha 1993, *The nation and its fragments: colonial and postcolonial histories*, Princeton, Princeton University Press, Princeton.

Chauvel, RH 1990, *Nationalists, soldiers and separatists: The Ambonese islands from colonialism to revolt, 1880–1950*, KITLV Press, Leiden.

Cheng, Shu-Ju Ada 2003, 'Rethinking the globalisation of domestic service: foreign domestics, state control and the politics of identity in Taiwan', *Gender & Society* 17(2).

Chin, CBN 1998, *In service and servitude: foreign female domestic workers and the Malaysian 'Modernity' project*, Columbia Press, New York.

Chiu, SWK 2005, 'Recent trends in migration movements and policies in Asia: Hong Kong region report', paper presented at Workshop on International Migration and Labour Market in Asia organised by the Japan Institute for Labour Policy and Training, Japan Institute of Labour, Tokyo, 20–21 January.

Clifford, J 1992, 'Travelling cultures', in Grossberg, L, C Nelson and P Treichler (eds), *Cultural Studies*, Routledge, London.

—— 1997, *Routes: Travel and translation in the late twentieth century*, Harvard University Press, Cambridge.

Cohen, R 2000 '"Mom is a stranger": the negative impact of immigration policies on the family life of Filipina domestic workers', *Canadian Ethnic Studies Journal* 32(3), accessed 10 May 2003.

Collier, WL, K Santoso, Soentoro and R Wibowo 1993, *New approach to rural development in Java: twenty five years of village studies in Java*, BPS Jakarta.

Constable, N 1997, *Maid to order in Hong Kong: stories of Filipina workers*, Cornell University Press, Ithaca.

—— 1999 'At home but not at home: Filipino narratives of ambivalent returns', *Cultural Anthropology* 14(2).

—— 2003, 'Filipina workers in Hong Kong homes: household rules and regulations', in Ehrenreich, B and AR Hochschild (eds), *Global woman: nannies, maids and sex workers in the new economy*, Granta Books, London.

Cox, S and P Carey 1995, *Generations of resistance: East Timor*, Cassell, London and New York.

CPCA 2004 '2004 Philippines elections update', *Kasama*, www.cpcabrisbane.org/Kasama/2003/V17n3/ElectionUpdate.htm, accessed 9 January 2005

Cummings, W 1998, 'The Melaka–Malay diaspora in Makassar, c1500–1669', *Journal of the Malayan Branch of the Royal Asiatic Society* 71.

Curtis, B and C Pajaczkowska 1994, '"Getting there": travel, time and narrative' in Robertson, G, M Mash, L Tickner, J Bird et al (eds), *Travellers' tales: narratives of home and displacement*, Routledge, London.

DIMIA (Department of Immigration, Multicultural and Indigenous Affairs), *Immigration Update*, various issues, AGPS, Canberra.

Domosh, M and K Morin 2003, 'Travels with feminist historical geography', *Gender, Place and Culture* 10(3).

Donohue, Mark 1995, 'The Tukang Besi language of Southeast Sulawesi, Indonesia', PhD thesis, Australian National University, Canberra.

DTK (Departemen Tenaga Kerja) 1998, *Strategi Penempatan Tenaga Kerja Indonesia Ke Luar Negeri*, Departemen Tenaga Kerja, Republic of Indonesia, Jakarta.

Duncan, J and D Gregory (eds) 1999, *Writes of passage: reading travel writing*, Routledge, London.

Dunn, J 1996, *East Timor: a people betrayed*, ABC Books, Sydney.

Echols, J and Hassan Shadily 1997, *Kamus Indonesia–Inggeris: an Indonesian–English dictionary*, 3rd ed, Gramedia, Jakarta.

eFilipinos 2005 *Pinoy Oversea*, www.efilipinos.com/forum, accessed 8 January 2005.

Ellerman, D 2003, Policy research on migration and development, http://econ. worldbank.org.

Elmhirst, R 2000, 'A Javanese diaspora? Gender and identity politics in Indonesia's transmigration resettlement program', *Women's Studies International Forum* 23(4).

Elshtain, JB 1992, *Just war theory*, Blackwell, Oxford.

—— 1993, 'Sovereignty, identity and sacrifice' in Ringrose, M and AJ Lerner (eds), *Reimagining the nation*, Open University Press, Buckingham.

EMPOWER 2003, *Voting rights for overseas Filipinos: campaign central*, www. philippineupdate.com/vote.htm, accessed 7 January 2005.

Enloe, CH 2000, *Bananas, beaches and bases: making feminist sense of international politics*, University of California Press, Berkeley and London.

Evers, H-D, W Clauss and S Gerke 1988, 'Population dynamics, ethnic relations and trade among Javanese transmigrants in East Kalimantan', Research Report Series No 48, Population Studies Center, Gajah Mada University.

Eviota, EU 1992, *The political economy of gender: women and the sexual division of labour in the Philippines*, Zed, London and Atlantic Highlands.

Exposto, E 1996, 'What it means to be East Timorese' in *It's time to lead the way: Timorese people speak about exile resistance and identity. Writings from a conference on Timor and its people*, East Timor Relief Association, Collingwood.

Ferguson, KE 1999, *The man question: visions of subjectivity in feminist theory*, University of California Press, Berkeley.

Firman, T 1991, Rural households, labour flows and the housing construction industry in Bandung, *Tijdschrift voor Economische en Sociale Geografie* 82(2).

Ford, M 2006, 'After Nunukan: the regulation of Indonesian migration to Malaysia' in Kaur, A and I Metcalfe (eds), *Mobility, labour migration and border controls in Asia*, Palgrave Macmillan, Basingstoke and New York.

Forth, G 1994, 'Considerations of "Keo" as an ethnographic category', *Oceania* 64(4).

—— 1998, *Beneath the volcano*, KITLV Press, Leiden.

Fox, JJ 1995, 'Foreword' in Southon, M, *The navel of the Perahu: Meaning and values in the maritime trading economy of a Butonese village*, Research School of Pacific and Asian Studies, Australian National University, Canberra.

—— 1997a, 'Place and landscape in comparative Austronesian perspective' in Fox, JJ (ed), *The poetic power of place: comparative perspectives on Austronesian ideas of locality*, Department of Anthropology, Research School of Pacific and Asian Studies, Australian National University, Canberra.

—— 1997b, 'Genealogy and topogeny: towards an ethnography of Rotinese ritual place names' in Fox, JJ (ed), *The poetic power of place: comparative perspectives on Austronesian ideas of locality*, Department of Anthropology, Research School of Pacific and Asian Studies, Australian National University, Canberra.

—— 2001, 'Asal dari mana? Departures and displacements' in Siikala J (ed), *Departures: how societies distribute their people*, TAFAS 46, Finnish Anthropological Society, Helsinki.

Fulcher, MB 1983, 'Resettlement and replacement: social dynamics in East Kalimantan, Indonesia', PhD thesis, Northwestern University.

Galuh Wandita 1991, unpublished tour report of visit to Lewoleba, Lembata, Flores Timur, Nusa Tenggara Timur.

Gennep, A van 1960, *The rites of passage*, Routledge and Kegan Paul, London.

Geschiere, P and B Meyer 1998, 'Globalisation and identity: Dialectics of flow and closure', *Development and Change* 29.

Gibson, K 2001, 'Regional subjection and becoming', *Environment and Planning D: Society and Space* 19.

Giddens, A 1990, *The consequences of modernity*, Stanford University Press, Stanford.

Global Nation 2005a, http://discussions.inq7.net/Forums/Thread, accessed 8 January 2005.

—— 2005b, http://www.inq7.net/globalnation/index.htm, accessed 7 January 2005.

GlobalPinoy.com 2005a, 'Global Filipinos', www.globalpinoy.com/, accessed 8 January 2005.

—— 2005b, www.globalpinoy.com/, accessed 7 January 2005.

Go, SP 2005, 'Recent trends in international movements and policies: the Philippines 2004', paper prepared for the Workshop on International Migration and Labour Markets in Asia organised by the Japan Institute of Labour, Tokyo, Japan, 21–22 January.

Gomes, D 1996, 'Resistance: twenty years of struggle supported by young East Timorese' in *It's time to lead the way: Timorese people speak about exile resistance and identity. Writings from a conference on Timor and its people*, East Timor Relief Association, Collingwood.

Graham, J 2002, 'Women and the politics of place: ruminations and responses', *Development* 45(1).

Graham, P 1994, 'Vouchsafing fecundity in eastern Flores: textiles and exchange in the rites of life' in Hamilton, R (ed), *The gift of the cotton maiden: textiles of Flores and the Solor islands*, Fowler Museum of Cultural History, University of California Los Angeles.

—— 1999, 'Seas that unite, mountains that divide: language, identity and development in Flores', *Anthropologi Indonesia* XXIII(58).

Grimes, B 1991 'The development and use of Ambonese Malay', *Pacific Linguistics* A-81.

Grimes, CE, T Therik, BD Grimes and M Jacob 1997, *A guide to the people and languages of Nusa Tenggara*, Artha Wacana, Kupang.

Guarnizo, LE and MP Smith 1998, 'The locations of transnationalism' in *Transnationalism From Below*, Transaction Publishers, New Brunswick.

Gunn, G 2000, 'The 500 year Timorese *Funu*', *Bulletin of Concerned Asian Scholars*, 32(1 and 2).

Gusmão, X 1999, 'Appeal by Xanana to Timorese', *TAPOL*, 1 March, www. easttimor.com/leaders/xanana_0020.html (accessed 19 April 2000).

—— 2000a, 'Maubere' in Niner, S (ed), *To resist is to win: the autobiography of Xanana Gusmão*, Aurora Books, Richmond.

—— 2000b, 'A history that beats in the *maubere* soul' in Niner, Sarah (ed), *To resist is to win: the autobiography of Xanana Gusmão*, Aurora Books, Richmond.

Hage, G 1993, 'Nation-building dwelling being', *Communal/Plural* 1.

Harcourt, W and A Escobar 2002, 'Women and the politics of place', *Development* 45(1).

Hardjono, JM 1977, *Transmigration in Indonesia*, Oxford University Press, Kuala Lumpur.

—— 1986, 'Transmigration: looking to the future', *Bulletin of Indonesian Economic Studies* 22(2).

Hassan, Hazlin 2004, 'Maids as slaves: Asia's hidden shame', the *Manila Times*, www.manilatimes.net/national/2004/jun/03/yehey/opinion/20040603opi7. html, accessed 21 January 2005.

Hatley, B 1997, 'Nation, "tradition", and constructions of the feminine in modern Indonesian literature' in Schiller, J and B Martin-Schiller (eds), *Imagining Indonesia: cultural politics and political culture*, Ohio Center for International Studies, Athens.

Henderson, G 1999, 'How much is East Timor worth to us?', *Age*, 23 February.

Hill, HM 1978, 'Fretilin: the origins, ideologies and strategies of a nationalist movement in East Timor', MA thesis, Monash University, Clayton.

Hobsbawm, Eric 1991, 'Exile: a keynote address—introduction', *Social Research* 58(1).

Hollander, John 1991, 'The idea of home: it all depends', *Social Research* 58(1).

House of Commons 2004, *Migration and development: How to make migration work for poverty reduction*, Stationery Office, United Kingdom.

Hugo, GJ 1975, 'Population mobility in West Java, Indonesia', PhD Thesis, Department of Demography, Australian National University, Canberra.

—— 1978, *Population mobility in West Java*, Gadjah Mada University Press, Yogyakarta.

—— 1980, 'Population movements in Indonesia during the colonial period' in Fox, JJ, RG Garnaut, T McCawley and JAC Mackie (eds), *Indonesia: Australian perspectives*, Research School of Pacific Studies, Australian National University, Canberra.

—— 1981, 'Levels, trends and patterns of urbanization', *Migration, urbanization and development in Indonesia,* Comparative study on migration, urbanization and development in the ESCAP region, Country Reports III, United Nations, New York.

—— 1987, 'Forgotten refugees: postwar forced migrations within Southeast Asian Countries', in Rogge, JR (ed), *Refugees: a Third World dilemma*, Rowman and Littlefield, Totowa.

—— 1992, 'Women on the move: changing patterns of population movement of women in Indonesia', in Chant, S (ed), *Gender and migration in developing countries*, Belhaven Press, London.

—— 1993a, 'Urbanisasi: Indonesia in transition', *Development Bulletin* 27, Australian Development Studies Network.

—— 1993b, 'Indonesian labour migration to Malaysia: trends and policy implications', *Southeast Asian Journal of Social Science* 21(1).

—— 1995, 'Labour export from Indonesia: an overview', *ASEAN Economic Bulletin* 12(2).

—— 1997, 'Changing patterns and processes in population mobility' in Jones, GW and TH Hull (eds), *Indonesia assessment: population and human resources*, Australian National University and Institute of Southeast Asian Studies, Canberra and Singapore.

—— 1998, 'International migration in Eastern Indonesia', paper prepared for East Indonesia Project, January.

—— 2000a, 'The impact of the crisis on internal population movement in Indonesia', *Bulletin of Indonesian Economic Studies* 36(2).

—— 2000b, 'The crisis and international population movements in Indonesia', *Asian and Pacific Migration Journal* 9(1).

—— 2000c, 'Labour migration from East Indonesia to East Malaysia: recent trends', *Revue Européene des migrations internationales* 16(1).

—— 2002a, 'Pengungsi – Indonesia's internally displaced persons', *Asian and Pacific Migration Journal* 11(3).

—— 2002b, 'Women's international labour migration' in Robinson, K and S Bessell (eds), *Women in Indonesia: gender, equity and development*, Institute of Southeast Asian Studies, Singapore.

—— 2003a, 'Migration and development : a perspective from Asia', *IOM Migration Research Series* 14.

—— 2003b, 'Information, exploitation and empowerment: the case of Indonesian contract workers overseas', *Asian and Pacific Migration Journal* 12(4).

—— 2005, 'Asian experiences with remittances' in Terry, DF and SR Wilson (eds), *Beyond small change: making migrant remittances count*, Inter-American Development Bank, Washington.

—— 2006a, 'Improving statistics on international migration in Asia', *International Statistical Review*, 74(3).

—— 2006b, 'Forced migration in Indonesia: historical perspectives', *Asian and Pacific Migration Journal* 15(1).

—— 2006c, 'Australian experience in skilled migration' in Kuptsch, C and Pang Eng Fong (eds), *Competing for global talent*, International Labour Organization (International Institute for Labour Studies), Geneva.

—— 2006d, 'Women, work and international migration in Southeast Asia: trends, patterns and policy' in Kaur, A and I Metcalfe (eds), *Mobility, labour migration and border controls in Asia*, Palgrave Macmillan, Basingstoke and New York.

Hugo, GJ, TH Hull, VJ Hull and GW Jones (eds) 1987, *The demographic dimension in Indonesian development*, Oxford University Press, New York.

Hull, TH, E Sulistyaningsih and GW Jones 1998, *Prostitution in Indonesia: its history and evolution*, Pustaka Sinar Harapan, Jakarta.

IBG (Institute of British Geographers) 1997, *Feminist geographies: explorations in diversity and difference*, Women and Geography Study Group, IBG and Longman Ltd, London.

ICG (International Crisis Group) 2001a 'Communal violence in Indonesia: lessons from Kalimantan', Asia Report 19, 27 June, www.crisisgroup.org/, accessed 19 May 2008.

—— 2001b 'Indonesia: natural resources and law enforcement', Asia Report 29, 20 December, www.crisisgroup.org/, accessed 19 May 2008.

—— 2005, 'Conflict history: Indonesia', www.crisisgroup.org/, accessed 19 May 2008

Ignacio, EN 2000, 'Ain't I a Filipino (woman)?: an analysis of authorship / authority through the construction of "Filipina" on the net', *The Sociological Quarterly* 41(4).

Ignatieff, M 1993, *Blood and belonging: journeys into the new nationalism*, Farrar, Straus and Giroux, New York.

Iguchi, Y 2000, 'The Japanese economy from recovery to rebirth – changes of the labour market and international migration', country report presented at Workshop on International Migration and Labour Markets in Asia, Japan Institute of Labour, Tokyo, Japan, 26–29 January.

—— 2005, 'Growing challenges for migration policy in Japan—to cope with regional integration and declining fertility', paper given at Workshop on International Migration and Labour Markets in Asia, Tokyo, 21–22 January.

Indonesian Observer 1995, 18 March.

Inside Indonesia 1996, 'Australians help codify Indonesian land titles', 47.

IOM (International Organisation for Migration) 2005, 'Engaging diasporas as development partners, for home and destination countries: a policy roadmap', workshop discussion paper, Mainstreaming Migration into Development Policy Agendas conference, Geneva, 2–3 February.

Jackson, M 1995, *At home in the world*, Duke University Press, Durham and London.

Jacobs, J and C Nash 2003, 'Too little, too much: cultural feminist geographies', *Gender, Place and Culture* 10(3).

Jayawardena, Kumari 1986, *Feminism and nationalism in the Third World*, Zed Books, London.

Johnson, B and S Sedaca 2004, *Diasporas, emigrés and development, economic linkages and programmatic responses*, A Special Study of the US Agency for International Development, Carana Corporation, March.

Jolliffe, J 1978, *East Timor: nationalism and colonialism*, University of Queensland Press, St Lucia.

Jones, GW 1995, 'Introduction', in Jones, GW and Y Raharjo (eds), *People, land and sea*, Demography Program, RSSS, Canberra.

—— 2004, 'Urbanization trends in Asia: the conceptual and definitional challenges' in Champion, A and G Hugo (eds), *New forms of urbanization*, Ashgate, Aldershot.

Jones, S 1995, 'First free trade—now for the free movement of labour', *Asiaview* 5(3).

—— 1996, 'Women feed Malaysian boom', *Inside Indonesia* 47.

—— 2000, *Making money off migrants: the Indonesian exodus to Malaysia*, Asia 2000 Ltd and Centre for Asia Pacific Social Transformation Studies, Hong Kong and Wollongong.

Kanapathy, V 2005, 'International migration and labour market developments in Asia: economic outlook, the labour market and migrant labour in Malaysia', paper prepared for the Workshop on International Migration and Labour Market in Asia organised by the Japan Institute for Labour Policy and Training, Tokyo, 20–21 January.

Kandiyoti, D 1998, 'Gender, power and contestation: rethinking bargaining with patriarchy', in Jackson, C and R Pearson (eds), *Feminist visions of development: gender analysis and policy*, Routledge, London.

Kapferer, B 1988, *Legends of people, myths of state: violence, intolerance and political culture in Sri Lanka and Australia*, Smithsonian Institution Press, Washington and London.

Kaur, A 2004, *Wage labour in Southeast Asia since 1840: globalisation, the international division of labour and labour transformations*, Palgrave Macmillan, Basingstoke and New York.

—— 2005, 'Indonesian migrant workers in Malaysia: from preferred migrants to "last to be hired"', *Review of Indonesian and Malaysian Affairs*, 39(2).

—— 2006, 'Order (and disorder) at the border: mobility, international labour migration and border controls in Southeast Asia' in Kaur, A and I Metcalfe (eds), *Mobility, labour migration and border controls in Asia*, Palgrave Macmillan, Basingstoke and New York.

—— 2007, 'International labour migration in Southeast Asia: governance of migration and women domestic workers', *Intersections: Gender, History and Culture in the Asian Context* 15.

Kearney, M 1991, 'Borders and boundaries of the state and self at the end of empire', *Journal of Historical Sociology* 4(1).

Kedit, PM 1980, *Modernization among the Iban of Sarawak*, Dewan Bahasa dan Pustaka, Kementerian Pelajaran Malaysia, Kuala Lumpur.

Keen, I 1994, *Knowledge and secrecy in an Aboriginal religion*, Clarendon Press, Oxford.

Kofman, E and K England 1997, 'Citizenship and international migration: taking account of gender, sexuality and "race"', *Environment and Planning A* 29(2).

Laurie, N, C Dwyer, S Holloway and F Smith, F (eds) 1999, *Geographies of new femininities*, Longman, New York.

Lawrence, KR 1994, *Penelope voyages: women and travel in the British literary tradition*, Cornell University Press, Ithaca.

Laws, G 1997, 'Women's life courses, spatial mobility, and policies', in Jones, JP III, HJ Nast and SM Roberts (eds), *Thresholds in feminist geography: difference, methodology, representation*, Rowman and Littlefield, Oxford.

Lawson, VA 1998, 'Hierarchical households and gendered migration in Latin America: feminist extensions to migration research', *Progress in Human Geography* 22(1).

—— 2000, 'Arguments within geographies of movement: the theoretical potential of migrants' stories', *Progress in Human Geography* 24(2).

Lee, JS 2005, 'Recent developments in Taiwan's economy and its labor market', paper presented at Workshop on International Migration and Labour Market in Asia organised by the Japan Institute for Labour Policy and Training, Japan Institute of Labour, Tokyo, 20–21 January.

Lineton, J 1975, 'An Indonesian society and its universe: a study of the Bugis of South Sulawesi (Celebes) and their role within a wider social and economic system', PhD thesis, School of Oriental and African Studies, University of London.

Llorito, D 2003, 'Consumption drives economy', the *Manila Times*, www. manilatimes.net/national/2003/aug/29/business/20030829bus1.html, accessed 9 January 2005.

Lucas, REB 2004, 'International migration regimes and economic development' paper presented at Third Co-ordination Meeting on International Migration Population Division, Population Division, Department of Economic and Social Affairs, United Nations, New York, 27–28 October.

Ma, Y 2005, 'Recent trends and data of economy, labor market and migration in China for 2005', country paper prepared for the Workshop on International Migration and Labour Market in Asia organised by the Japan Institute for Labour Policy and Training, Japan Institute of Labour, Tokyo, 20–21 January.

Magenda, B 1989, 'The surviving aristocracy in Indonesia: politics in three provinces of the outer islands', PhD thesis, Cornell University.

Malkki, LH 1992, 'National geographic: the rooting of peoples and the territorialization of national identity among scholars and refugees', *Cultural Anthropology* 7(1).

—— 1995a, 'Refugees and exile: from "Refugee Studies" to the national order of things', *Annual Review of Anthropology* 24.

—— 1995b, *Purity and exile: violence, memory and national cosmology among Hutu refugees in Tanzania*, University of Chicago Press, Chicago.

Mallett, S 2004, 'Understanding home: a critical review of the literature', *Sociological Review* 52(1).

Manning, C 1998, *Indonesian labour in transition: an East Asian success story?*, Cambridge University Press, Cambridge.

Mantra, IB, TM Kasnawi and Sukamardi 1986, *Mobilitas Angkatan Kerja Indonesia Ke Timur Tengah [Movement of Indonesian workers to the Middle East]*, Final Report Book 1, Population Studies Centre, Gadjah Mada University, Yogyakarta.

Marcus, GE and M Fischer 1986, *Anthropology as cultural critique*, University of Chicago Press, Chicago.

Martin, P 2004, *Migration and development: toward sustainable solutions*, International Institute for Labour Studies Discussion Paper DP153/2004, Geneva.

Martin, PY 1992, 'Gender, interaction, and inequality in organisation' in Ridgeway, CL (ed), *Gender, interaction, and inequality*, Springer-Verlag, New York.

McClintock, A 1993, 'Family feuds: gender, nationalism and the family', *Feminist Review* 44, Summer.

McDowell, L 1999, *Gender, identity and place: understanding feminist geography*, Polity Press, Minneapolis.

McDowell, L and JP Sharp (eds) 1997, *Space, gender, knowledge: feminist readings*, Arnold, New York and London.

MI (Migrante International) 2005 *Campaigns, June 7: Migrants' Day*, www. migrante.org/content/campaigns_mem/june03/june7_migday_ gma.htm, accessed 7 January 2005.

Miller WG 1980, 'An account of trade patterns in the Banda Sea in 1797, from an unpublished manuscript in the India Office Library', *Indonesia Circle* 23.

Minh-ha, TT 1994, 'Other than myself/my other self', in Robertson, G, M Mash, L Tickner, J Bird et al (eds), *Travellers' tales: narratives of home and displacement*, Routledge, London.

Mok, Quentiliano 1996, 'The role of RENETIL: national resistance of East Timorese students' in *It's time to lead the way: Timorese people speak about exile resistance and identity. Writings from a conference on Timor and its people*, East Timor Relief Association, Collingwood.

Mubyarto, 2000, *Indonesia's transmigration program: experience and prospect*, JCAS Symposium Series 10, Japan Center for Area Studies, National Museum of Ethnology, Osaka.

Newland, K 2004, *Beyond remittances: the role of diasporas in poverty reduction in their countries of origin. A scoping study by the Migration Policy Institute*, Department of International Development, Washington.

Nguyen, NX 2003, 'International migration of highly skilled workers in Vietnam', paper presented at the Workshop on International Migration and Labour Markets in Asia, Japan Institute of Labour, Tokyo, 4–5 February.

Niner, S (ed) 2000a, *To resist is to win: the autobiography of Xanana Gusmão*, Aurora Books, Richmond.

—— 2000b, 'A long journey of resistance: the origins and the struggle of the CNRT', *Bulletin of Concerned Asian Scholars*, 32(1 and 2).

Nonini, D 2002, 'Transnational migrants, globalisation processes, and regimes of power and knowledge', *Critical Asian Studies* 34(1).

Nonini, D and A Ong 1997, 'Introduction: Chinese transnationalism as an alternative modernity', in *Ungrounded empires: the cultural politics of modern Chinese transnationalism*, Routledge, New York and London.

Noorduyn, J 1991, *A critical survey of studies on the languages of Sulawesi*, KITLV Press, Leiden.

Norval, A J 1996, 'Thinking identities: Against a theory of ethnicity' in Wilmsen, EN and P McAllister (eds), *The politics of difference: ethnic premises in a world of power*, University of Chicago Press, Chicago.

Oey-Gardiner, M 1997, 'Educational developments, achievements and challenges' in Jones, GW and T Hull (eds), *Indonesia assessment: population and human resources*, Institute of Southeast Asian Studies, Singapore.

OFWO (Overseas Filipino Workers Online) 2005a, www.theofwonline.com/forum/default.asp, accessed 8 January 2005.

—— 2005b, www.theofwonline.com/, accessed 8 January 2005.

Pannell, S 2003, 'Violence, society and the state in eastern Indonesia: context' in Pannell S (ed), *A state of emergency: violence, society and the state in eastern Indonesia*, Northern Territory University Press, Darwin.

Park, Y 2005, 'Country report: Korea', paper presented at Workshop on International Migration and Labour Market in Asia organised by the Japan Institute for Labour Policy and Training, Japan Institute of Labour, Tokyo, 20–21 January.

Parreñas, RS 2001a, *Servants of globalisation*, Stanford University Press, Stanford.

—— 2001b, 'Transgressing the nation-state: the partial citizenship and 'imagined (global) community' of migrant Filipina domestic workers', *Signs* 26(4).

—— 2003, 'The care crisis in the Philippines: children and transnational families in the new global economy', in Ehrenreich, B and AR Hochschild, *Global woman: nannies, maids and sex workers in the new economy*, Granta Books, London.

Parta, MN 1996, 'Karakteristik Pedagagang Kaki Lima Suku Bugis: Studi Kasus di Pasar Citra Niaga Kotamadya Samarinda', thesis, Program Pasca Sarjana Universitas Padjadjaran.

PDLE (Philippines Department of Labor and Employment) 2004, 'Bagong Bayani Awards launched today', *DOLE News*, Manila, online, www.dole.gov.ph/news/pressreleases2004/june04/176.htm, accessed 7 January 2004.

Pelras, C 1996, *The Bugis*, Blackwell, Oxford.

Peluso, NL 1987, 'Merchant, manipulation, and minor forest product on the Mahakam: Bugis political economic strategies in pre-colonial Kutai', International Workshop on Indonesian Studies No 2, Royal Institute of Linguistics and Anthropology, Leiden, 2–6 November.

—— 2006, 'Passing the red bowl: creating community identity through violence in West Kalimantan, 1967–1997' in Coppel, CA (ed), *Violent conflicts in Indonesia: analysis, representation, resolution*, Routledge, London and New York.

Penny, JL 1993, 'Indonesians in Australia: from migration to integration 1947–1986', PhD thesis, LaTrobe University, Bundoora.

Penny, JL and Siew-Ean Khoo 1996, *Intermarriage: a study of migration and integration*, Bureau of Immigration and Multicultural Research, Melbourne.

Pettman, JJ 1996, *Worlding women: a feminist international politics*, Allen & Unwin, St Leonards.

Philstar.com 2005, www.philstar.com/philstar/index.htm, accessed 8 January 2005.

Pile, S and N Thrift (eds) 1995, *Mapping the subject: geographies of cultural transformation*, Routledge, London.

Pillai, P 1992, *People on the move: an overview of recent immigration and emigration in Malaysia*, Institute of Strategic and International Studies, Kuala Lumpur.

—— 1995, 'Malaysia', *ASEAN Economic Bulletin* 12(2).

Pinto, C and M Jardine 1997, *East Timor's unfinished struggle: inside the Timorese resistance*, South End Press, Boston.

Piper, N 2003, 'Feminization of labor migration as violence against women: international, regional, and local nongovernmental organization responses in Asia', *Violence Against Women* 9(6).

POEA (Philippines Overseas Employment Administration) 2002, *Deployment of newly hired OFWs by skills category 1992–2002*, www.poea.gov.ph/html/statistics.html, accessed 21 January 2005.

—— 2003, *Stock estimates on Philippines overseas workers, as at December 2003*, www.poea.gov.ph/html/statistics.html, accessed 7 January 2005.

—— 2004, *The Bagong Bayani Awards 2005*, www.poea.gov.ph/html/bba2005.html, accessed 7 January 2005.

Poerwadarminta, WJS 1976, *Kamus umum Bahasa Indonesia*, Balai Pustaka, Jakarta.

Poole, R 1985, 'Gender and national identity', *Intervention* 19.

PPK (Pusat Penelitian Kependudukan) 1986, *Mobilitas Angkatan Kerja ke Timur Tengah*, Gadjah Mada University, Yogyakarta.

Pramono, DS 2000, *Penangan Internally Displaced Persons (IDPs) Sebagai Akibat Terjadinya Konflik Sosial dengan Tindak Kekerasan. Makalah disampaikan dalam Simposium Nasional Pokok-Pokok Masalah Kebijakan Terkini Mengenai Mobilitas Penduduk Urbanisasi dan Transmigrasi*, Jakarta, 25–26 May.

Pratt, ML 1992, *Imperial eyes: travel writing and transculturation*, Routledge, London.

Proxy-Maid (no date), *All about maid*, www.proxy-maid.com.hk/, accessed 18 January 2005.

Pujiastuti, TN 2000, 'The experience of female overseas contract workers from Indonesia', MA thesis, Department of Geographical and Environmental Studies, University of Adelaide.

Raj-Hashim, R 1994, 'A review of migration and labour policies' in Heyzer, N, GL à Nijeholt and N Weerakoon, *The trade in domestic workers: causes, mechanisms and consequences of international migration*, Zed Books, London.

Ramos-Horta, J 1987, *Funu: The unfinished saga of East Timor*, Red Sea Press, Trenton.

—— 1999, 'The first steps on Timor's long road back', the *Age*, 2 December.

Reuter, T 2006, 'Land and territory in the Austronesian world' in Reuter, T (ed), *Sharing the earth, dividing the land: land and territory in the Austronesian world*, ANU EPress, Canberra.

RI (Republic of Indonesia) 1993, *Indonesia: a quarter century of progress, 1968—1993, tables and graphs*, Jakarta.

Rival, L (ed) 1998, *The social life of trees: anthropological perspectives on tree symbolism*, Berg, Oxford and New York.

Robertson, G, M Mash, L Tickner, J Bird et al (eds) 1994, *Travellers' tales: narrative of home and displacement*, Routledge.

Robinson, J 2000, 'Power as friendship: spatiality, femininity and "noisy surveillance"' in Sharp, JP, P Routledge, C Philo and R Paddison (eds), *Entanglements of power: geographies of domination/resistance*, Routledge, London.

RP (Republic of the Philippines) 2005a, *OFW Portion*, www.gov.ph/forum, accessed 8 January 2005.

—— 2005b, www.gov.ph/, accessed 8 January 2005.

Rumbaut, RG 1997, 'Assimilation and its discontents: Between rhetoric and reality', *International Migration Review*, 31(4).

Rykwert, J 1991, 'The idea of home: house and home', *Social Research* 58(1).

Sassen, S 1998, 'Notes on the incorporation of third world women into wage-labour through immigration and off-shore production' in *Globalisation and its discontents*, The New Press, New York.

—— 2003, 'Global cities and survival circuits' in Ehrenreich, B and AR Hochschild (eds), *Global woman: nannies, maids and sex workers in the new economy*, Granta Books, London.

Scenes from an occupation 1999, video recording, Carmela Baranowska, Viagen Films, Laburnum, Victoria.

Sharp, JP, P Routledge, C Philo and R Paddison (eds) 2000, *Entanglements of power: geographies of domination/resistance*, Routledge, London.

Silvey, R and V Lawson 1999, 'Placing migrant', *Annals of the Association of American Geographers* 89(1).

Silvey, RM 2000, 'Stigmatized spaces: gender and mobility under crisis in South Sulawesi, Indonesia', *Gender, Place and Culture* 7(2).

Singhanetra-Renard, A 1986, *The Middle East and beyond: dynamics of international labour circulation among Southeast Asian workers*, mimeo.

Soeprobo, TB 2005, 'Recent trends in international migration in Indonesia', paper prepared for Workshop on International Migration and Labour Market in Asia organised by the Japan Institute for Labour Policy and Training, Japan Institute of Labour, Tokyo, 20–21 January.

SooBong Uh 2000, 'Immigration and labour market issues in Korea', country report prepared for Workshop on International Migration and Labour Markets in Asia, Japan Institute of Labour, Tokyo, Japan, 26–29 January.

Southon, M 1995, *The navel of the Perahu: Meaning and values in the maritime trading economy of a Butonese village*, Research School of Pacific and Asian Studies, Australian National University, Canberra.

Spaan, E 1999, *Labour circulation and socioeconomic transformation: the case of East Java, Indonesia*, Report 56, NIDI, The Hague.

Srivastava, S 2005, '*Ghummakkads*, a woman's place, and the LTC-walas: towards a critical history of "home", "belonging" and "attachment"', *Contributions to Indian Sociology* 39(3).

Stacey, J 1997, 'Can there be a feminist ethnography?' in McDowell, L and JP Sharp (eds), *Space, gender, knowledge: feminist readings*, Arnold, New York.

Standing, Guy 1998, 'Global feminisation through flexible labour', in Jameson, KP and CK Wilber (eds), *The political economy of development and underdevelopment*, Sixth edition, McGraw Hill, New York.

Strathern, M 1991, *Partial connections*, Rowman and Littlefield, Savage.

Sunaryanto, H 1998, 'Female labour migration to Bekasi, Indonesia: determinants and consequences', PhD thesis, Population and Human Resources, University of Adelaide.

Suryakusuma, JI 1996, 'The state and sexuality in New Order Indonesia' in Sears, LJ (ed), *Fantasizing the feminine in Indonesia*, Duke University Press, Durham.

Suyono, M 1981, 'Tenaga Kerja Indonesia di Timur Tengah Makin Mantap', *Suara Karya*.

Tadjoeddin, MZ 2002, 'Anatomy of social violence in the context of transition: the case of Indonesia 1990–2001', Working Paper 02/01-E, United Nations Support Facility for Indonesian Recovery, Jakarta.

Tambiah, SJ 1996, 'The nation-state in crisis and the rise of ethnonationalism' in Wilmsen, EN and P McAllister (eds), *The politics of difference: ethnic premises in a world of power*, University of Chicago Press, Chicago and London.

Taylor, JG 1999, *East Timor: the price of freedom*, Pluto Press, Annandale.

Thomas, PS 2003, 'Philippines: whereto for overseas Filipino workers?', *Asia Pacific*, Radio Australia, Interviewed by Kanaha Sabapathy, www.abc.net.au/ra/asiapac/programs/s930300.htm, accessed 22 August 2003.

Tippet, Gary 1999, 'Hail the poet warrior', the *Age*, 5 November.

Tirtosudarmo, R 1997, 'Economic development, migration, and ethnic conflict in Indonesia: a preliminary observation', *Sojourn – Journal of Social Issues in Southeast Asia* 12(12).

—— 1998, 'Demography and security: the transmigration policy in Indonesia', seminar paper, *Demography and Security*, MIT, Boston, 11–12 December.

—— 2004, 'Cross-border migration in Indonesia and the Nunukan tragedy', in Ananta, A and EN Arifin (eds), *International migration in Southeast Asia*, Institute of Southeast Asian Studies, Singapore.

Traube, E 1995, 'Mambai perspectives on colonialism and decolonisation' in Carey, P and GC Bentley (eds), *East Timor at the crossroads: the forging of a nation*, Cassell, London.

Tregonning, KG 1965, *A history of modern Sabah (North Borneo 1881–1963)*, 2nd edition, University of Malaya Press, Singapore and Kuala Lumpur.

Tsing, AL 1993, *In the realm of the diamond queen: marginality in an out-of-the-way place*, Princeton University Press, Princeton.

Tule, P 2004, *Longing for the house of God, dwelling in the house of the ancestors: local belief, Christianity, and Islam among the Keo of Central Flores*, Academic Press, Freibourg.

Turner, V 1969, *The ritual process: structure and anti-structure*, Aldine, Chicago.

Valentijn, F 1858, *Oud en Nieuw Oost-Indien*, HC Susan, 's Gravenhage.

Van de Wall, VI 1934, 'Bijdrage tot de geschiedenis der perkerniers 1621–1671', *Overgedrukt uit het Tijdschrift voor Ind. Taal-, Land- en Volkenkunde* 146.

Verdery, K 1996, 'Whither nation and "nationalism"?' in Balakrishnan, Gopal (ed), *Mapping the nation*, Verso, London.

Wahyuni, ES 2000, 'The impact of migration upon family structure and functioning in Java', PhD thesis, Department of Geographical and Environmental Studies, University of Adelaide.

Walby, S 1996, 'Woman and nation' in Balakrishnan, G (ed), *Mapping the nation*, Verso, London.

Wang Gungwu 1985, 'Migration patterns in history: Malaysia and the region', *Journal of the Malayan Branch of the Royal Asiatic Society* 58.

Wee, V and A Sim 2004, 'Transnational networks in female labour imgration' in Ananta, A and EN Arifin (eds), *International migration in Southeast Asia*, Institute of Southeast Asian Studies, Singapore.

Werbner, P 2004, 'The predicament of diaspora and millennial Islam: reflections on September 11, 2001', *Ethnicities* 4(4).

Wilkes, J 1995, 'The social construction of a caring career', in Burck, BSC (ed), *Gender, power and relationship*, Routledge, London.

Williams, CP 2007, *Maiden voyages: eastern Indonesian women on the move*, KITLV Press, Leiden and Institute of Southeast Asian Studies, Singapore.

Wilson, E 1991, *The sphinx in the city: urban life, the control of disorder, and women*, Virago, London.

WIN (Women's International Network) 1995, 'Women in the workforce: a global review 1985–1995', *WIN News* 21(3).

Winn, P 1998, 'Banda the blessed land—sacred practice and identity in the Banda Islands', *Antropologi Indonesia* 57.

—— 2001, 'Graves, groves and gardens: Place and identity—central Maluku, Indonesia', *Asia Pacific Journal of Anthropology* 1(2).

—— 2002, 'Banda the blessed land: local identification and morality in a Maluku Muslim community', PhD thesis, Australian National University, Canberra.

—— 2003, 'Sovereign violence, moral authority and the Maluku *cakalele*' in Pannell S (ed), *A state of emergency: violence, society and the state in eastern Indonesia*, Northern Territory University Press, Darwin.

Wood, WB 1985, 'Intermediate cities in the resource frontier: a case study of Samarinda and Balikpapan, East Kalimantan, Indonesia', PhD thesis, University of Hawaii.

World Bank Group 2003, *Philippines data profile*, www.worldbank.org, accessed 19 August 2003.

Yap, MT 2005, 'Singapore country report', paper prepared for the Workshop on International Migration and Labour Market in Asia organised by the Japan Institute for Labour Policy and Training, Japan Institute of Labour, Tokyo, 20–21 January.

Yeoh, BSA and S Huang 1999a, 'Singapore women and foreign domestic workers: negotiating domestic work and motherhood' in Momsen, JH (ed), *Gender, migration and domestic service*, Routledge, London.

—— 1999b, 'Spaces at the margins: migrant domestic workers and the development of civil society in Singapore', *Environment and Planning A* 31(7).

—— 2000, '"Home" and "away": foreign domestic workers and negotiations of diasporic identity in Singapore', *Women's Studies International Forum* 23(4).

Yuval-Davis, N 2001, 'Nationalism, feminism and gender relations' in Guibernau, M and J Hutchinson (eds), *Understanding nationalism*, Polity Press, Cambridge.

Zarembka, JM 2003, 'America's dirty work: migrant maids and modern-day slavery' in Ehrenreich, B and AR Hochschild (eds), *Global woman: nannies, maids and sex workers in the new economy*, Granta Books, London.